REDEFINING MANHOOD

MANHOOD

A Guide for Men and Those Who Love Them

REDEFINING MANHOOD

A Guide for Men and Those Who Love Them

Jim PathFinder Ewing
(Nvnehi Awatisgi)

FINDHORN PRESS

The right of Jim PathFinder Ewing to be identified as the
author of this work has been asserted by him in accordance
with the Copyright, Designs and Patents Act 1998.

Published in 2015 by Findhorn Press, Scotland

ISBN 978-1-84409-660-2

Edited by Nicky Leach
Illustrations by Annette Waya Ewing
Cover and Interior design by Damian Keenan
Printed and bound in the USA

Published by
Findhorn Press
117-121 High Street,
Forres IV36 1AB,
Scotland, UK

t +44 (0)1309 690582
f +44 (0)131 777 2711
e info@findhornpress.com
www.findhornpress.com

Dedication

To our fathers,
to our mothers;
To the child within,
Who becomes our father
and our mother,
Who we are,
And who our children,
and our children's children
Will be.

Epigraph

As Children of Earth and Sky,
there is no him or her or me;
All is a Circle.
It always comes around to us.

Contents

Preface

In your hands is the seventh book in the PathFinder series. The series started with a book entitled *Clearing: A Guide to Liberating Energies Trapped in Buildings and Lands*. That book, the first in a trilogy on spiritual issues, was followed by *Finding Sanctuary in Nature: Simple Ceremonies in the Native American Tradition for Healing Yourself and Others*, and *Healing Plants and Animals From a Distance: Curative Principles and Applications*. All three are related to environmental shamanism--a way of practicing shamanism that unites us with our surroundings and helps us reconnect to our natural selves.

Next came two books on Reiki Shamanism: *Reiki Shamanism: A Guide to Out of Body Healing*, which combines Reiki with shamanism, and the fifth book, *Dreams of the Reiki Shaman: Expanding Your Healing Power*.

The first Reiki Shamanism book came about because I was teaching a new way of practicing shamanism, by combining it with Reiki, the art of hands-on healing, and people were inquiring as to how to go about it. The second, which I sometimes refer to as essentially Volume Two of Reiki Shamanism, came about in response to questions from students regarding this modality that were not included in the first book. I've since taught dozens of students how to combine these modalities, in my home, in classes on the road, and at Kripalu Center for Yoga and Health, where I've been honored to be invited as guest faculty. *Dreams of the Reiki Shaman* also expands on ways of seeing, or methods of perceiving the world, incorporating traditional Native American teachings as well as visionary practices from other disciplines beyond traditional shamanism.

The book before this one is entitled *Conscious Food: Sustainable Growing, Spiritual Eating*, and it arose from operating a farm using organic growing methods. It explores how our society became divorced from the spiritual aspects of growing food and supplying nourishment for society. It seeks to answer the questions: When did growing and eating food cease to be considered sacred? How did food lose its connection with health? Why is our food system out of control?

Many of the concepts in the book you hold in your hands were derived from the research into writing *Conscious Food*, including the fact, in the words of one historian, that women "invented" agriculture. It is a realm that has become almost exclusively male in the industrial model, even as a robust food movement embracing organic, fresh, local, and nutritious foods is turning the industry upside down, promoted and supported by young women and shared by supportive young men.

This equalization of food production, distribution, and promotion away from the dominating hierarchical patriarchal models is the equivalent of the 1960s peace movement, as fundamental and life-altering as it is persistent and culture-changing. It is only one aspect of changing culture back to indigenous matrifocal belief systems. The same forces that made patriarchal societies wrest control of food and growing from matriarchal societies—thereby transforming the growing and distribution of food from a sacred act providing nourishment to whole societies into a weapon of war creating fear, lack, division, and domination—also changed the definitions and roles of men and women. Society now seems to be coming full circle to a postmodern equality of sexes.

This book came about because of repeated requests for a retreat on men and men's issues, similar to the classes I've held over the previous decade on other aspects of healing, health, and spirit. I wrote it with the intention of using it in a class for and about men, but I hope that it will be of interest and value to both men and women. This is why I have called it *Redefining Manhood: A Guide for Men and Those Who Love them.*

Men are responsible for their own evolution, but so are women. It remains true that "the hand that rocks the cradle rules the world," and women have a say in how men are reared from infancy; the credit, or blame, is a shared one. Moreover, the influence of women in men's lives, from boyhood to adolescence to manhood, cannot be underestimated—not only mothers, sisters, aunts, and cousins but significant others: lovers, girlfriends, wives, and daughters.

My hope is that this book will prompt searching and substantive discussions about what it means to be a man. The ultimate goal is to shift understandings and behaviors to a kinder, gentler, more thoughtful and compassionate model, and away from the stubborn, anti-intellectual, dogmatic, insensitive one so largely found in popular culture, which seems to promote inappropriate thoughts, beliefs, and behaviors.

A theme throughout my books has been the importance of maintaining a balance between the inner male and female. We each have these voices within us. They are qualities that are typically categorized as male or female, but in our society the masculine is emphasized to the exclusion of the female in men, while the feminine is emphasized to the exclusion of the male in women.

Things are changing, but as the impetus toward same-sex marriage and the dashing of female stereotypes has taken center stage in Western society, the role of the male has been muddied and confused. Is that bad? I don't think so. Rather, I think it offers a wonderful opportunity to rethink manhood, taking into account changing roles, changing mores, and changing demands on the male half of the human equation.

This is not a "man's movement" book. It's not designed or intended to make men "more like" men or "against" feminism. Nor is it designed to make men "more like" women or "for" feminism (although I admit a bias in favor of feminist thought in viewing the skewed nature of our society, applauding the research feminist writers and thinkers have brought to light, and the need to bring balance in male/female relations). Rather, this book recognizes an essential fact that has been clearly understood by most cultures on the earth prior to the modern age, in traditional indigenous societies around the world—that men and women are human beings first.

That is the impetus of this book: how to make men, all of us, better human beings. It doesn't matter whether we are considered "masculine" or "feminine," or neither, or have a gender orientation one way or another—anyone can benefit from reading and using this book. Indeed, I hope that all kinds of people—male and female, and of diverse orientations—will find this book helpful in their personal relationships with others and, most important, with themselves.

On The Structure of the Book

The book is divided into three chapters:

- The first chapter explains why I wrote this book. The role of men in society has become so muddled and confused that one author has gone so far as to proclaim "The End of Men," with respect to our usefulness and value. This chapter discusses how the archetypes that have served as models for men no longer apply.

- The second chapter explores how our views on men, and men's relations with others in the world, became so skewed. I review thousands of years of history, including the subversion by the Romans of early Christianity, and detail the forces today that are making those views obsolete.

- The third chapter delves deeper into obsolete archetypes and suggests traits that should be emphasized in male development (both children and adults), based on age-old indigenous practices, and qualities that are positive and useful to men, women, and society.

I have included exercises at the end of each chapter to help you master key concepts. I encourage you to keep a notebook of your own observations for inner discovery; I have provided entries from my own notebook as examples.

As with previous books, the end of each chapter includes key words that may be searched on the Internet to allow you to gain greater understanding. You can access the web directly if you are reading an e-book version and using a smart device. All of my books are currently available in Kindle, Nook, Sony, and iPad readable text.

The book concludes with a glossary of useful terms, notes, and a bibliography of publications that offer a foundation in understanding men's roles and personal development in today's world. In addition, our website *Healing the Earth/Ourselves*, at www.blueskywaters.com, offers additional reading material that may be ordered, as well as information about periodic workshops. This book is by no means definitive on the subject of men or male/female relationship.

As in previous books, "healing" is defined as finding wholeness and balance—in the way that was taught to me and not through being cured by Western allopathic medicine. "Medicine" is defined as the intrinsic power within a thing to be whole. Nothing in this book, or in my previous books, should be construed as offering medical advice.

My intention with this book is to offer men (and their significant others) a guide that I hope may prove instrumental in thinking about what it means to be a man, with the goal of self-defining manhood in a positive way. In doing so, I recognize (and outline) that relationships are all over the map. While the media focuses on the extremes—especially the drumbeat of fundamentalists trying to legislate their narrow views into laws the government would enforce—I hope to bring attention to the social experiments enacted daily by individuals seeking and choosing their own "families," creating loving relationships in which they give and find acceptance and in which they find a sense of belonging. Somewhere between the old order that's not working and the new order that's emerging, men will hopefully find a place to call home.

May you find many blessings on this path!

Introduction

The Child is the Father
If we do not redefine manhood, war is inevitable.
— PAUL FUSSELL

I heard his voice as if from another planet: "Get up! Get up! You're okay. Get up!" It wasn't said with love, but with fear and anger, and shouted at me.

My father had been drinking heavily. We were out on the patio. I was too young to really know what drinking was, but I knew what it did to my father: it made him mean, someone to be feared, and avoided.

I had walked out to the patio before our guests arrived. I had gone to ask my father something. I was seven. He was sitting in a lawn chair on the patio, drinking beer. I don't know what I said to set him off, but he shouted at me, "Don't be sneaking up on me like that!" Then wham! His open hand came down upon my head. Apparently, my father's wedding band connected with my skull and knocked me senseless. I fell on the concrete face first.

Next thing I knew, I was floating in darkness.

I was weeping in this void. "I can't take this anymore," I sobbed to the inky vastness. A warm voice came back, illuminating the darkness, so full of life it sounded like water in a time of thirst: "You won't have to endure such pain much longer. Things will get better."

"I'm ready to go, now!" I wailed, knowing with my child's inner knowing that, yes, this was a true exit point where I could choose to leave my body for good.

Instead of my life flashing before my eyes, this nourishing voice, this unseen angel, showed me scenes of my life to come: pleasant and wondrous visions: of falling in love, driving a car, and even having a child of my own. "These are things you have to look forward to," said the voice, so full of love and caring, caressing me with its words.

"It's your choice," the voice said. "You can choose to leave now. But you will miss many good things that you will wish you had stayed to see and feel."

Reluctantly, vowing that I would never treat a child as I had been treated, I came back to the frantic, angry, and fearful voice of my father, who kept shouting at me that I wasn't hurt.

Sobbing, I rolled on my back and tried to get up. Between lips split and bloody, I said with a quavering, resolute voice: "Stop hitting me."

He picked me up in his arms, this big, strong, powerful man, and held me tight, his alcohol breath like kerosene, his unshaved face like sandpaper against my soft wet cheek, vowing he would never hit me again. And I knew then that it wasn't he who had been hitting me, but his father who had hit him as a child, and his father before him. And I knew I had to break the cycle.

This book is a way to nourish that little child—in you, in me, in your children, so no one has to live that way again.

Needed — A New Model for Our Sons, Grandsons, and Ourselves

The sins of the father are to be laid upon the children.
— *WILLIAM SHAKESPEARE, THE MERCHANT OF VENICE*

I wrote this book because my friend Alison Buehler had asked repeatedly for me to teach a men's retreat to complement the women's retreat she sponsored at the Mississippi Modern Homestead Center in Starkville, Mississippi. I had declined for several reasons. Foremost, I told her, if I taught a retreat, I would want to do it right. That meant more than merely regurgitating what others in the genre have taught. And that's for a reason, too: I don't believe most of what is written. Mainly, that's because I think it's based on the wrong model.

Most books on the subject—and courses—are based on the same stereotypes that our society promotes of the "strong" human or the warrior, or conversely, they mirror women's retreats, where the male is supposed to be more like women. These retreats often incorporate concepts and activities that are Native American in origin, including the pipe fast (or vision quest), talking stick, drumming, and other techniques.[1]

That's logical, since it makes sense to look at indigenous ways, and the role of men in indigenous societies, to understand what is truly fundamental in men's roles without the veneer of modern life.

While I agree with and heartily endorse Native American con-cepts and carefully guided activities, and include some of them in this book, the framework that commonly is promoted with these activities in men's retreats is fundamentally flawed. The cultural con-text from which these activities occurred is exactly opposite from current mainstream society; moreover, the philosophy behind such spiritual tools is overlooked entirely, so their use and validity are sub-stantially diminished.

Simply put: Native America, with few exceptions, was tradition-ally matrilineal or matrifocal—that is, mothers headed families—not patriarchal, as is the case with our Western society.

The importance of this cannot be stressed enough. In Eastern American tribes especially, all property belonged to the female, and decision making was done by the clans, or family units, headed by the females. Taking rituals that arose from Native American societies and trying to impose them on a patriarchal society removes much of the meaning from them. So, while not rendered useless, the tools often used in men's retreats and treatments of men's roles are of lim-ited scope when it comes to gender identity. With some moderation, such tools are perfectly suited for use by both males *and* females, but in Native societies, they were primarily the province of the male in a cultural milieu where women were the major decision makers.

Traditionally, these rituals were as powerful for males as the men-strual hut was for the female surrounded by her female relatives. Each was a gender-specific ritual that meant initiation into adult-hood for the male and female, respectively, in a primarily matrilineal society.

Both were steeped in a complex of ideas that are diametrically at odds with prevailing Western thought. This includes emphasis on cooperation and sharing, rather than control and domination; recog-nition of differences as strengths, rather than oddities or weaknesses;

building self-reliance based on a spiritual connection to Earth and its beings (especially the supernatural and the nonrational), rather than objectifying, exploiting, and dominating Earth and its beings, seen and unseen; adherence to a belief system that abundance, not scarcity and lack, is the will of Creation; and finally, definition of wealth to mean how much is given and shared, rather than how much is taken or kept.

There are still further differences when it comes to applying Native spiritual technologies to modern life. Men in Native America needed to be taught harsh reality at an early age because life was physically hard, filled with the very real consequences of behavior— if a young man could not hunt or endure the rigors of want or battle, his usefulness to the tribe was limited. So, the pipe fast, or spirit quest, was a hard physical endurance test, as was the sweat lodge, in the context of male coming-of-age ceremonies. Those qualities are not the same as those required for life in modern Western society. Nor do women have the exalted status that females had in Native America, where they would inherit all the property, make all the important tribal decisions, and choose the men who would represent and carry out their interests.

In its entirety, the Western way of viewing the world is upside down and backwards to traditional indigenous belief systems. To try to cherry pick a few rituals to instill goals that modern society wants to promote while ignoring the context in which those rituals arose is to limit their effectiveness. Worse, trying to attach Western meanings to these rituals without the spiritual ideas that underlie them robs them of their true spiritual power.

Beyond these considerations (as if they weren't enough), the natural state of Native American tribes was not war but peace. (I use the term Native American to mean American Indians of North America.) In all of the Eastern tribes, at least, the polarity of war and peace was sharply observed. There was the white path and there was the red path; there was a white, or peace, chief and a red, or war, chief. In times of peace, this white chief was the leader and executive of the tribe; during war, a war chief was elected to carry out the essential tasks required. As soon as the war was over, the peace chief regained control. Red chiefs were usually men; white chiefs could be either men or women.

This belief system extends across tribes and regions in various forms, going back thousands of years to ancient beliefs about the Thunder Twins, or giants of the earth, who played stickball to determine the fate of humankind. It exemplifies the dual nature of life: hot, cold; up, down; yes, no; light, darkness—the yin/yang of all things upon this world.

It recognized that there would be times of joy and times of grief, times of ease and times of hardship, times of war and times of peace, and that men and women, and whole tribes, including the young and elderly, would seek to survive come what may as a unit, without division, sharing in all tasks. But it also presupposed that the natural aspiration of humankind is toward life, not death; toward goodness, not fear, pain, or hate; and that the goal of human beings is to do good, in peace and harmony, not wage war. That belief system, of "right relationship" with Creator, Earth, and all beings, is fundamental to traditional Native American spirituality in all its expressions.

In the modern day, this fundamental characteristic of traditional Native American belief and practice is totally ignored, while also trivialized to promote an idea that everything "Indian" is good. It homogenizes tribal differences to a Pan-Indianism that creates false, idealistic, and even fantastic views of tribal life, destroys historical accuracy, and obliterates important regional and historical cultural differences that are inimical to homogenization.

It's not helped by the fact that much of what is thought to be "Native American" is in fact, a product of the war chief mentality and status. That's understandable, since Native America has been under attack and almost wiped out during the last two centuries. As a result, most of what is remembered and handed down by the descendants of indigenous people are songs and stories of war. But that was not the daily or even common reality of Native America for millennia before Europeans came.

While war is a constant in human history, peace is the goal; it is the natural state that allows societies around the world to flourish. The conditions that lead naturally to a stable, happy, healthy, and prosperous society are peace, unity, sharing, cohesiveness, recognizing individual strengths and weaknesses, and utilizing those differences for the common good—not war and domination.

So, at heart, all the retreats, workshops, and trainings about the role of men seeking, in ways large and small, to honor the inner "warrior" as a Native American belief are based on a flawed concept—as flawed as the misunderstanding of Native America as it exists today, and as flawed even as the misunderstanding of European history for millennia until the Romans spread their patriarchal warrior ways (and gods).[2]

If the ideas and concepts commonly used in men's retreats and trainings are backward, misapplied, misunderstood, or inappropriate, is all hope lost for finding a spiritual path for men in the modern age? Not by any means. Studying Native American and other indigenous (including pre-Roman European) practices is still important, as these practices can offer role models for male behavior and provide valuable tools and resources for redefining manhood in the modern age. But one must first start from a different premise: that men are both unique *and* share qualities and traits with women.

Finding "right relationship" for men—with God, planet, other beings, including humans male and female—is a way of peace, not of warfare. That bears repeating: The natural state of men is one of peace—not war, not violence, nor the threat of violence, but a system of living that ensures peace and avoids disruption. It is a way of finding and nourishing traits that grow love, compassion, respect, and understanding, not division, eradication, and domination. We share our planet and our lives with love, compassion, and responsibility, including wisdom, resolve, and empathy; we do not dominate our world with wanton destruction, anger, hate, fear, division, and exploitation, treating other beings, including women, as objects.

The strength of the male is not his potential fearsomeness (war or warrior energy) nor his female side (which is important and should be nurtured) but his unique ability to blend the two to become a father, brother, uncle, son, friend, and lover, with love and respect for himself and those around him as a way of peace, as a matter of choice. To hold up a warrior's path or "iron" countenance without the true mettle of peace, love, and compassion is to create a two-dimensional figure. It is a caricature of men, one that does not recognize the unique strengths and abilities of being a man in a relationship that exalts his manhood.

I could not find a guide for such a concept, I told Alison, and therefore could not offer such a workshop or even a book for her to read.

But, she said, "I want something to teach my boys!"

Against that mother's plea, I had no answer. Rather than a barrier, it became a challenge. What can I give to Alison's boys? Indeed, what can I give to my own son and my grandson? What is the path for peace in the training of men? How can men be whole?

First, an overview.

Stages of a Man's Life

One of most enlightening books on where men are today is written from a Christian perspective, a book entitled *The Stages of a Man's Life* by E. James Wilder. It breaks down the subject of men as men by life stages and relationships. They include: Man as Brother, Man as Friend, Man as Priest, Man as Lover, Man as Warrior, Man as King, Man as Husband, Man as Servant. It goes on to devote more pages to Man as Father and, sure to excite some dissent, Man as Father to His Wife, among other subchapters. The book is filled with wonderful insights and anecdotes about male-female relationships and contains a great deal of wisdom.

Wilder's view may harken more to an earlier era when relationship roles were more sharply defined by gender, and still may hold sway among those who follow fundamentalist Christian faiths. Nonetheless, it's useful as a personal tool to review stages in one's life and determine causative agents. Exercises are included in this book to explore the individual's formative agents and events.

However, influences alone aren't enough to fix one's relationships or provide a new way of viewing the world. One must recognize that massive changes are taking place in the world today that affect the way relationship roles are being played out. That's what makes relying on role models and former examples of manhood confusing and no longer as certain as before.

We cannot begin to redefine manhood to meet modern needs without also examining the very real forces at play that are changing traditional male/female roles and the demands on families today. Integral to that is the fact that men are both the oppressors and the oppressed, as harsh as that sounds. Men perpetuate a system in their personal lives and the world around them that supports war and division—and domination. The "angry white male" is angry for a reason.

You might ask: If white males (and increasing numbers of black males and white women) are in power and the oppressors, then why are they so angry? The answer is simple: they feel powerless. Why?

In their book, *From Wild Man to Wise Man: Reflections on Male Spirituality*, Father Richard Rohr, OFM Fr., a Franciscan of the New Mexico province, and Joseph Martos, a theologian and retired professor of religious studies, blame the hierarchical system of society. Every man has a boss who has a boss who has a boss in the hierarchy. The stresses of always meeting someone else's deadlines and expectations take their toll, they say. Most men have very little power or autonomy in their work life or family life, in many instances. If they are not trying to please bosses, they are trying to please customers, or trying to please family members who want a new car or want to go on a vacation, or some other additional expense. Or they worry about the institutions with sway over them, such as the bank that holds their mortgage and credit card debt, or decides their credit worthiness so that they can buy a house or buy a car; or they worry about those on the job who have a say in whether they get a promotion and higher pay or are fired. Even top executives are told what to do by company policies or boards of directors or market forces beyond their control. This lack of control makes them simultaneously passive and angry.

Our culture gives men the illusion of control and provides white men with fallacies that guide their behavior, including that they are superior and expected to control others. But this is an illusion and its conflict with reality, Rohr and Martos write, undermines and victimizes men. It teaches men to oppress, as they are themselves oppressed by the system. Hence, men's liberation, they say, is more difficult than women's liberation. Women know they are oppressed, and that is the first step in liberation. Men in our culture have just enough middle class limited freedom and marginal wealth to not fully appreciate their lack of choices and how they are duped. As more and more women surpass men in income, earning capability, and economic attainment, however, the biblical shingles may be pulled from their eyes. This goes to the very heart of what it means to be a man, and the much more subtle role of masculinity in modern society.

What is the relationship between manhood and masculinity? Are they synonymous? As Todd W. Reeser, a professor at the University of Pittsburgh who teaches gender studies, notes in his book, *Masculinities in Theory: An Introduction*, there are several traits that people commonly associate with masculinity. "Muscular," "hard," "brave," and "in control" are words often used, he says, that are generally deemed the opposite of femininity. Adjectives that do not describe masculinity include "weak," "soft," and "emotional." (These are often stereotypes and prejudices hurled at women.) Masculinity may be associated with body-builders or men eager for a fight, Reeser says.

But manhood adds another dimension to roles and responsibilities. Masculinity can be a statement without being spoken. For example, a leader may invade a country, and the fact that he is male is understood, as part of the "package," if you will. As French theorist Roland Barthes writes, the unmarked term—gender attached to violent behavior—is not an absence of meaning but "a significant absence." The silence speaks.[3]

As Reeser says, this absence of "mark" distinguishing the speaker's gender, thought to be not gendered (when it's intrinsic to the decision and decision maker), may say more about the qualities of masculinity and its ubiquity in society than if it were noted. By contrast, how would this fact of a gendered characteristic be noted if the leader were female or gay? It is itself a "mark" of our Western society, and a hidden hurdle for women seeking positions of authority.

Manhood, however, is not intrinsic to the idea of the male or a salient characteristic. Manhood is defined by action, by behavior, by tests, roles, and relationships. A man can be masculine and not pass the test of manhood by, say, war or other definition. Modern societies as well as ancient ones had tests of manhood. A boy, however masculine in appearance, could not be accepted as a man by his peers or other men until he had been initiated. Masculinity is a quality of men to a greater or lesser degree, and manhood is comprised of the qualities that are expected of a man, as measured by roles, tests, and achievements.

The types of initiations are tied to qualities that are prized in the specific society. A Maasai male in tribal society might have to kill a lion on the African plains to be accepted as a man in the men's hut. In America, a young man's invitation to the local Lion's Club could signify the same, qualified by earning enough money to make a life on his own, obtaining an academic degree, starting a business, getting married or having children.

Masculinity is defined by stated and unstated descriptions of appearance and behavior; manhood is defined by relationships. With society rapidly changing, the forces that distinguish men among men are also rapidly changing. The benchmarks are shifting. We must look at where men are coming from in the definitions of men in society, and where women are going, to see how yin and yang no longer jibe. Manhood must be redefined to be meaningful, or it will become as meaningless as a Maasai warrior looking for a lion to kill in New York's Central Park.

As Hanna Rosin notes in *The End of Men: And the Rise of Women*, men and women in modern society have reached the end of thousands of years of human history in the way economic forces have shaped families and are at the start of a new era. As reported extensively, the shift in economic roles was accelerated by the Great

Recession of 2008, which hit men much harder than women: three-quarters of the 7.5 million jobs lost were held by men. Those manufacturing jobs are not coming back, and it merely accelerated a trend already underway for the past 30 years.

In 2009, for the first time in American history, the balance of the workforce tipped toward women, who had held half of the nation's jobs. The United Kingdom and several other countries hit the tipping point a year later, Rosin notes. And that trend is accelerating.

For decades, women have outpaced men in the number of postsecondary degrees conferred, earning nearly 10 million more college degrees than men in the past 20 years. But, in 2010, women started to surpass men in attainment of degrees higher than a bachelor's degree, as well. The growing divide is striking: For every 100 men who graduate with a college degree in 2015, 140 women will do the same.

This has helped narrow the gender pay gap, according to research from the Pew Research Center. Millennial women (women aged 18 to 32) now make almost as much money as their male peers. And it has rearranged gender norms: 21 percent of married women in 2012 had husbands who were less educated than they were. According to census data, the disparity was most striking between African-American and Hispanic women and their mates.

Some researchers want to refute the figures, noting that the top executive posts are still overwhelmingly in the hands of men. That's because it is men who choose who enters the executive suite. According to *Catalyst*, women currently hold only 5 percent of Fortune 500 CEO positions and 4.9 percent of Fortune 1000 CEO positions. *The New York Times* observed that women make up only 16 percent of directors at Fortune 500 companies and 10 percent of chief financial officers at S.& P. 500 companies.[4]

But that's not the full picture. Women hold a majority (51.4 percent) of all management, professional, and related jobs. There's a pent-up surplus of qualified female employees waiting for executive suite jobs. As educational disparities continue, and a tipping point is reached, those nearly exclusively male figures are sure to crumble. It should also be noted that once women break through the "glass ceiling," those scaling the heights of corporate America tend to have compensation packages that are as jaw-droppingly gigantic as men at a similar level.[5]

The trend toward greater female advancement is expected to continue. As more women attain more education and higher-paying jobs, and at an earlier age, their earning capacity and wealth should continue to accelerate. This situation has already reached a tipping point in gender roles. As Rosin notes, why should women rely on men for their basic economic needs? The answer for many young women is that they aren't. Men may be useful at times, but they are no longer an economic necessity, nor does society automatically value men as highly as it once did.

Popular culture is reflecting this shift.

In her 2011 song *"Run the World (Girls),"* rock diva Beyoncé celebrates the rising role of women in a pop anthem of sorts, rhetorically asking, "Who runs the world?" and repeatedly exclaiming in the refrain, "Girls!"

For an even greater "Hear Me Roar" message, Iowa Republican state senator Joni Ernst blew away her opponents in a five-way U.S. Senate primary on June 6, 2014, winning with 56 percent of the vote and beating her nearest opponent by 38 percentage points. It was based in no small part on her TV advertisement, entitled "Squeal," in which she detailed how her experience castrating pigs as an Iowa farm girl would help her "cut pork" in Washington. The message was no doubt received, as well, that the U.S. Senate is one of the last bastions of predominantly male hierarchy. She reiterated that pledge during her victory speech.

If there is a "battle of the sexes," it appears that women have won, even if the casualties (and gains like pay equality) are still being tallied.

But the war analogy is not helpful, nor has it ever been. It is the product of a patriarchal view in which conflicts are resolved by physical strength (the male forte), and a new paradigm is needed. The shift underway should not be considered or be allowed to devolve into a zero sum game or everyone loses. As is taught in traditional indigenous societies, seeing one gender as "less than" weakens the whole.

Failed Figures of Male Self-Identity

As if the current social and economic prognosis of men in society weren't unsettling enough, social theorists believe, with good authority, that the major influences that have served to shape men's lives are flawed.

All men can look back at the figures who provided the most instruction or influence when they were growing up. It starts with the father, even if it's a father in absentia, and continues through a variety of role models and figures in authority, including many women. Indeed, some authors say there are too many women raising boys, which keeps them from becoming men; they lack adult male role models and, hence, stay trapped in adolescent mindsets that treat women like objects in relationships characterized by rebellious selfishness. Conversely, there is a prevailing view among male gender theorists that all men today are fatherless in our society because of a lack of mentorship, whether their fathers are physically present or not. It's a cycle called "the father wound."

The Dark Mother

In his book, *Toward Manhood: The Wilderness of the Soul,* Larry Pesavento goes into detail about this "father wound" of absent men in the lives of male children, whether it's a physical absence in the home or a mental and emotional absence. He describes the pernicious effects of men who, in turn, fail to become men as a result of living a life dominated by "the dark mother." It is a voice or imperative that teaches men to be unconscious and passive, to be self-indulgent and hide secrets. It creates shame and fosters denial. It's this mindset that causes men to perpetuate horrors and not accept blame but blame others, pretending that their excesses were alternatively not worth notice or were merited by circumstances, however fanciful or self-serving. It creates addictions and insulates men from their emotions and from each other, thus perpetuating the wound and its effects on men and society.

In Pesavento's view, only a warrior mentality with a sword of truth can cut through the dark mother energy. He gives true-life stories of dysfunctional relationships handed down through generations, from father to son, because of this complex. It breeds absent fathers, if present at all, more bent on their careers than attending to parenting, and leads to sons enacting the dreams of their fathers and not their own because of it. This father wound, the void of real love and honest emotion between fathers and sons, he says, makes men distrustful of other men, innately worried that they are rivals for the dark mother's energy.

Pesavento calls the father wound epidemic in our society, providing a faulty model or training manual for fatherhood. Like original sin, it's visited upon the generations from father to son without end, unless something comes along to break the cycle. He is sympathetic, saying that there are no bad guys, and most fathers do their best, but the wound exists. Seeing our fathers as brothers in pain and darkness is a way to cut through the dark mother's energy. In the absence of a strong father figure, boys and young men pick up on the patriarchy of society to mold them; they become victims perpetuating their own woundedness. By this estimation, all men are victims of the sins of the fathers, as the Bible tells it, visited generation upon generation. They live their lives in darkness, unable to see themselves and each other as victims and, hence, continue to victimize each other.

Where Did It Begin?
The Supposed Loss of the Wild Man

In his seminal work, *Iron John: A Book About Men*, Robert Bly traces the history of the Wild Man, counterpart to the goddesses of Europe prior to AD 1100. He disappears just as Christianity becomes the bride companion of secular power throughout Europe, a process started about AD 1, when Caesar invaded Gaul. He traces the earliest origins of the Wild Man, Forest Lord, or Master of Animals to the Sumerian epic *Gilgamesh*. Bly sees the domestication of Enkidu, the wild hairy man, as a vital energy that was lost—an innate respect for maleness that lost its divine status. What Bly asserts may be true, to an extent, but it cannot be seen in isolation. It is coupled with the loss the divine feminine, as well; Gilgamesh only looks at one side: the masculine. It is true and valid, but only half the story.

The Epic of Gilgamesh
Sets Archetypes for Male Domination

The importance of this legend to the evolution of the concept of manhood in Western civilization cannot be overlooked. It shares the essential tenets of the Bible's Old Testament, which forms the basis of Christian, Jewish, and Islamic thought. In both The Garden of Eden and The Epic of Gilgamesh, a man is created from earth by divine power and lives in a wild, unconscious state with animals. He is tempted by a woman—there is even a snake present, which steals immortality, and an epic flood that few survive. In both stories, the woman offers him food and knowledge, invites him to leave his wild home, and he finds himself unable to resume his wild state. The following is a summary: [6]

Gilgamesh, a ruler of earthly power, was created by the gods as a god and one-third man. He was the ruler of Uruk and strongest of all the land. He ruled with cruelty, raping maidens, kidnapping young men for war, even children, disregarding the pleas of the aged. Anu, the god of Uruk, heard their prayers and sought help from Aruru, the goddess of Creation. She dipped her hands in clay and fashioned a man of wildness, Enkidu, a man with long hair that waved like that of the goddess of corn. He ate grass with the gazelle and ran with them. One day, a hunter saw him and was afraid. He told his father that this man was strongest in the world, an immortal from heaven. The father alerted Gilgamesh.

Upon hearing of this, Gilgamesh told the hunter to take a harlot from the temple and strip her naked and let the wild man see her comely figure at the watering place he frequented, so that he would be subdued. The hunter did as Gilgamesh told him, and after three days, Enkidu showed up with a herd of gazelle. The woman saw Enkidu and bared herself and made him welcome. For six days and seven nights they shared their bodies. But when Enkidu was satisfied and left her, the gazelle fled from him. His body was weakened, and he could not catch up with them. So, he returned to the woman and sat at her feet and listened to her extol the virtues of the city. Hearing her words, he realized he was alone and lonely and welcomed the comradeship of men.

"Why do you want to run wild with the beasts?" she asked him. "I will take you to Uruk, and you will meet Gilgamesh, the strongest of men."

Enkidu welcomed this idea, proclaiming that he was born of the goddesses and was oldest of the hills and would subdue this Gilgamesh in a feat of strength.

When they met, Gilgamesh defeated Enkidu in a wrestling match. They became comrades and went on a quest together, with Gilgamesh seeking immortality. The gods decided Enkidu must die, and Gilgamesh grieved over the death of his friend.

As outlined in my previous book, *Conscious Food: Sustainable Growing, Spiritual Eating*, this clash between Enkidu, the wild hairy man, and Gilgamesh, the ruthless patriarchal ruler, heralded the change from nomadic society to the settled civilizations with the birth of agriculture.

The Epic of Gilgamesh (from the Third Dynasty of Ur, 2150–2000 BCE), the oldest known major work of literature, can be seen as an example of an agricultural/warrior society, in which the goddess culture that had previously ruled was conquered.

For most of known human history and prehistory, Spirit has been identified as a feminine power (from at least 25,000 BCE), which found its highest expression with the founding and development of settled agriculture. Farming started the neolithic revolution about 12,000 years ago in the Middle East, with the domestication of goats and sheep and the discovery that certain grains could be planted and harvested.

The oldest known town in which farming and hunting/gathering (paleolithic) peoples coexisted was Catal Huyuk on the coast in southern Turkey. Agriculture began there with cultivation of barley around 8000 BCE, and the two ways lived side by side for about 2,000 years. Around 6000 BCE, people began moving to the river valleys, where agriculture became the principle food source around 5800 BCE. Thus, *The Epic of Gilgamesh* seeks to explain this shift in fabled lore.

Settled societies revolutionized human behavior and, from their earliest origins, deepened the cultural/religious connections with land. Thus, the womb (earth/soil) becomes sacred space, from which arises the temple, where is offered up the safety of society as a cooperative whole, along with its premier archetypes of home/culture/civilization.

By the time of *Gilgamesh*, the role of the feminine as divine was preeminent, and respect for living things was a crucial element of nature, from nurture in the cradle to seedlings in the ground to admiration of the human form in full maturity, without shame. Such holistic culture was goddess culture. But *Gilgamesh* foretells another stirring that was gaining force: with the rise of patriarchal nation-states based on the food surplus created by farming, the exalted role of women and the balance between men and women in society began to crumble.

It's noteworthy in this story that a "harlot" was taken from the temple to the fields. That completely turns upside down the cultural milieu of the goddess culture, in which sexual activity was seen as sacred and ritualized by ceremonies consecrating the land by maidens in the goddesses' employ. By the time of Classical Greece, in the writings of Homer and Hesiod in the eighth and ninth centuries BCE, woman were increasingly being considered property and spoils of war. Male storm gods or thunder gods came to displace goddesses as objects of veneration. These gods represented male power and violence, with war the guiding theme, as epitomized by the *Gilgamesh* point of view.

Men came to see themselves as masters over nature and women, ruling the nation-states that depended on agriculture and extending their military power to conquer others. Agricultural communities in matriarchal societies saw themselves as a part of nature; patriarchal nation-states that arose from agricultural communities saw themselves above nature, dominating and ruling it (her) and became "as" god. The spiritual connection between land, Spirit, and human beings weakened, with agriculture becoming a product of human will and not a spiritual collaboration.

In her ground-breaking book, *The Chalice and the Blade*, Riane Eisler writes that civilization shifted to a "dominator" model, in which one half of humanity is ranked over another. In *Conscious Food*, I explore this history and its repercussions to the modern day, including the rising food movement as counter to this historical theme.

Similarly, holistic medicine is a typically non-masculine way of looking at the world. When viewing things holistically, the causative agent of an illness, disease, disorder, or what-have-you may not be apparent or even discernible, nor its treatment rationally explained. The typical Western model, when it cannot explain something, rejects it, even if it works. Hence, such time-proven and effective treatments as found in traditional Chinese medicine, such as acupuncture, which is thousands of years old and routinely used by a significant portion of the population of the earth, is considered unfounded fakery, quackery, or inexplicable by strict Western logic. (For more on holistic medicine techniques and philosophy, see *Finding Sanctuary in Nature: Simple Ceremonies for Healing Yourself and Others*, and *Reiki Shamanism: A Guide to Out of Body Healing*.)

Rather than, as Bly suggests, something essentially masculine and male being lost with the seduction of Enkidu (unless you see it from the dominator model point of view), Enkidu is recruited into the warrior hierarchy and made part of the system of kingship and patriarchal power. Rather than the preexisting culture of goddesses showing man his inner goodness and celebrating his maleness, Enkidu is now lured to promote the idea that maidens of the temple are the property of men, prostitutes to be enslaved and used, not divine, autonomous, self-reliant architects of their own fate.

Enkidu wrestles with the hierarchy, but by then the battle is over: he is seduced by the lure of power over women as willing slaves to his desire, and he is conquered by the overwhelming might of the patriarchal, hierarchical military/industrial complex as it existed then. Then as now, that is focused on domination and subjugation, trades in food (nourishment), Spirit (a conqueror's religion), and men (the crushing of individuality to provide soldiers willing to sacrifice their lives to the system) to reward the top while subsisting off the bottom, the weak, and women.

The Epic of Gilgamesh is a perfect metaphor for modern man—one that is reenacted every day. Enkidu is born free, learns that he can't live without a paycheck, is hired by Gilgamesh, gives his all to the corporate-industrial-warfare system, and is killed by it, ushered to a premature grave after failing to build a family and a home life that he loves. Gilgamesh grieves but moves on; the corporation endures. Graveyards are filled with indispensable men like Enkidu.

Seeing Enkidu as something men have "lost" is only half the story; it's based on old archetypes that exalt the wild nature of men— men as warriors, a separate class from women. In *Iron John*, Bly says that real men have within them a "natural brutality" and much of what most people would consider cooperation and collaboration between men and women—for the sake of family and society, for example—he considers "naïve."

That view inevitably perpetuates and justifies all the excesses of patriarchy and warlike civilization. It should be apparent that such a mindset is guaranteed to create mixed-up young men, insensitive and brutish adult males, and a skewed corporate/military/industrial society that has marginalized women and others who do not subscribe to that view (or who cannot physically, mentally, or ethically cope with it) as second-class citizens and, hence, expendable.

According to the "Iron John" way of looking at manhood, as Bly says, a man who is not naïve must learn to live with "the dark side of God." To be a man, one not only doesn't flinch from such pain, he expects it, invites it, doesn't see life as whole and complete without it. He scoffs at "descent" from man's lofty manly perch as "kitchen work," and says every man is cursed by the dark side of the Great Mother as an "enraged woman," or one who causes him to suffer her inconsistency or betrayal. According to Bly, the "war" extends to women, and all things womanly, as well. (For more on this line of reasoning, see historian Robert S. McElvaine's *Eve's Seed: Biology, the Sexes and the Course of History*, which traces the history of men blaming women for men's excesses.)

The Iron John approach is precisely the wrong way for men to view women and men in this changing world we live in, and men who indulge such ancient hates will become increasingly isolated and rendered irrelevant. Such views really do spell the "end of men," a downward spiral that must be shifted, for the sake of men and women, our families, and our society.

How do we change this generational cycle of darkness and pain, loss and void?

Pesavento would probably recoil from the idea as antithetical to his view, but perhaps it's time to allow some female energy to shed light on this life cycle (extending the biblical "sins of the father are visited on the son" analogy), allowing the fruit of knowledge to be extended so that both male and female can banish this curse to the darkness from which it came. Let "Dark Mother" be dark no more. Let men become men, not perpetual adolescents. Let the "father wound" heal with inner nourishment that is shared among the whole family: mother, father, child, and all their relations. It can be done. It starts with the individual.

EXERCISE 1: *Stages of a Man's Life*

A useful method for assessing one's path as a man is to see it as stages in life.

Who were your role models growing up, and why? What did they teach you? When you hear yourself think, whose voice is it? Your father's? A teacher's? A military drill instructor? Or some other authority figure? Is that voice male? Determine and describe these "directors" in your life.

At what age did you become an adolescent? What was your idea of a man's role and responsibilities?

At what age did you marry (or have your first long-term, meaningful relationship)? What was your idea of a man's role and responsibilities?

At what age did you have children (or assume a role in which other people view you as a teacher or role model)? What was your idea of a man's role and responsibilities?

What qualities do you see now as the most important to you as a man? Are you happy about who you have become? If you had it to do over, based on your experience, what would you do differently (or teach to your children or grandchildren or young people)?

EXERCISE 2: *Manhood Defined by Relationship*

Briefly characterize your different roles and rate your satisfaction for each, using the following labels (as many as apply to you). To the best of your knowledge, how do your roles differ from those of your father? If you rate your satisfaction or effectiveness as low, how would, or should, you improve or change? If there is something you believe is keeping you from changing, what is it? Is it something that can be changed, and how?

- Man as Brother
- Man as Friend
- Man as Lover
- Man as Husband
- Man as Father
- Man as Cooperator, Counselor, Moderator
- Man as Spiritual Leader
- Man as Peacemaker

Finally, what are your descriptions of masculinity and manhood? How do they differ. What are the defining characteristics of becoming a man? Are these the same as for your father? For your son?

EXERCISE 3: *What's Your Style?*

Men and women often telegraph their interests, personas, or pretensions through their style of clothing. It's true that the *Fortune 500* CEO might on occasion dress like a pool boy or a garage mechanic might "clean up real good" in a Brooks Brothers suit. It's true too that our clothing and our interests may not coincide, except by necessity. Still, designers speak of one's "look" or style.

Ralph Lauren, for example, has its Black Label, Purple Label, or Polo, described by *The New York Times* as representing every conceivable American type: the Hollywood glamour boy, the Newport clubman, the Montana rancher, the Honolulu beach boy, the Nebraska trucker, the California easy rider, the Montauk surfer, the Connecticut preppy, the Nantucket trustafarian, among others.[7] The newspaper notes that casual wear is coming to be more distinctive and personal, even in the workplace, more of a statement than a utilitarian function among men.

What's your look? What does it say about you? Does it reflect who you really are? Is it something you crafted yourself or merely adopted? If so, when? As a child? As an adult? When? Why?

Who were the men—and women—in your life who contributed to this look? List them. For example, perhaps it was your father or favorite uncle who wore workpants or shoes like the ones your wear today, or a wife or girlfriend who said you looked good in a certain type of clothing.

Were your style models people on TV, in movies, magazines, and so forth? Who were they? What did this "look" say about them, about you?

Perhaps it's time to try something new, to reflect the new you, your unique style?

EXERCISE 4: *The Power of Recapitulation*

In shamanism, a powerful way to reshape one's "self" is through a practice called "recapitulation." Although it has been used in many societies in many different ways, the purpose of recapitulation is to release past emotional baggage, disengage memory "loops" that keep us repeating old lessons that may not have even been true when they were learned, and release us from behavioral patterns that have outserved their usefulness.

One way involves taking an inventory of who you "think" you are, and the influencers who shaped your thinking, and remake those assumptions and understandings.

For example, if you had an angry mother figure, you would write down memories and associations with your mother. Presumably, they would be of her being angry. Now, write down loving moments, caring moments, moments of insight and support—however few and fleeting they might be. Remember these good points and accurately assess: She may have been angry sometimes, but she also was _____

_____

(note whatever the act, statement, behavior was that was beneficial and brings to mind positive attributes).

As you focus on these positive attributes, you will begin to see that your mother wasn't "evil" or "angry," per se, but that she was at times angry and hard to deal with, and you will see that she also was, at times, loving and compassionate.

The key is changing your perception of your mother, or whoever the figure might be. You may never know why another person acted as they did, but if you catalog positive qualities, you will see that this person was just a person, with faults like any other person. Look then for the positive lessons you learned, even if they were survival issues. These perceptions of yourself and the significant other then become the significant ones, not the ideas, beliefs, memories, and fears that you have carried around with you since childhood or from the time of the influencer's contact with you.

Through recapitulation, you learn mastery of who you "think" you are. Mind you, this is not who you really are. When you hear yourself thinking "I am this, and I am not that" or "I would never do that" or "I shouldn't do that," and other such formative and behavior modifying instructions, that's not who you truly are. Those are the voices of the influencers in your life that you have internalized. That is who you "think" you are, and that determines your behavior. Rather, who you really are is the one who listens to these voices and acts. This book attempts to connect you with who you really are and, hence, changes your behavior to reflect your authentic self.

From the Author's Notebook

Recapitulation and the Lawn Mowing Incident

RECAPITULATION is a great way of unraveling guilt, anger, embarrassment, shame, and other negative emotions from swirling in your conscious, or just below it, and staving off the repetition of conducive behaviors and associations.

As an example, I can point to an incident when I was 10 years old and how it repeated itself three decades later (and probably many more times I was not aware of).

When I was a boy, I had a lawn-mowing business. At the time, I charged $3.50 to mow an average lawn in our neighborhood (about a half-acre). This was the same price as my competition, there being a sort of understood order to these things in the neighborhood. That would normally take me about two hours and half a tank of gas.

One day, I came home from school and my mother said that she had arranged for me to mow the lawn of a woman who was moving away. I asked the usual questions: Where is it? How big is it? And so on. My mother said that she had agreed for me to mow it for $3. I said that was below my price. Not only that, but it was really in someone else's neighborhood, about a mile away—a long way for a 10-year-old to push his lawnmower to "work," mow the lawn, and push it back. I told her my charge was at least $5 for such a task, or it wasn't worth my time and effort.

My mother told me that it was an elderly woman and I should do it as a favor; old people need to be cared for, and she probably couldn't afford much more. This appealed to my sense of fairness and ethics, even though I was begrudging about not being able to broker my own deal. The kicker was that the elderly woman's son was waiting for me at the house and I needed to hop to it. So, I changed clothes, filled up the lawnmower with gas, and made the long trek.

When I got there, though, the situation was different. The elderly woman had moved and had apparently been gone from the abandoned house for some time; in addition, the yard was overgrown with grass up to my knees—not a simple mowing but a physical ordeal for a 10-year-old boy with a push mower. To top it all, the yard wasn't just a yard but a double lot (built on two lots)! This yard would have been more suited for older boys working in tandem with bigger equipment and charging $10.

In fact, the "son" was there—a bald, middle aged, cigar-smoking tyrant who couldn't contain his glee at how cheaply he was getting the job done. I had no doubt that he had called all those who mowed lawns in the neighborhood and had been turned down for trying to pay next to nothing for it, only finding a sucker with me and my mother.

He gave me the $3 and said he was going out of town and would be back to make sure it was done. I tried to tell the man that this wasn't a $3 job. He turned angry and berated me, saying a deal was a deal, and if you agree to do a job you have to do the job.

I gave it my best shot. I mowed until I ran out of gas, then I pushed the mower home. It was a Friday, and I returned the next day and mowed until I ran out of gas again. This was the equivalent of four mowings normally. The third day, Sunday, I said to myself that I had had it. This wasn't fair. I wasn't making any money—now I was only paying for my gas. So I stayed home and didn't mow the last quarter of the yard in the back. I was embarrassed and ashamed and angry, but I had had enough.

About a week later, the man called my mother and complained that I had not done the job. Then he came over and stood at our front door. My mother called me and I came and looked up at this angry man. I lied to his face. Yes, I mowed your yard, I said.

He said that he would have to hire someone else to mow the lawn, and I acted like this offended me, that I was sorry, but I was trying to hide my glee and relief. He stormed away, shooting me angry looks as he left.

My mother was concerned. She took his side. "Jim, did you not mow that man's yard as you said you would?" I lied again. I mowed his yard, I said (which was true—just not all of it). I guess the rain has caused it to grow up again. (Which was also true, as it had rained during the week.) But, of course, I didn't speak the truth, and I felt shame mixed with anger.

This event stayed with me. For one thing, I raised my rates. I told my mother that my new rate was $5 per yard and that I would not agree to do any yard without looking at it first. Period. As it turned out, that was fine with most of my regular patrons; in fact, with some of the larger yards I got up to $7.50. I mowed fewer yards but made more money, and some of those who balked at $5 came around later.

Fast-forward 30 years. I'm married and we are having some flooding issues in the backyard at our house. A neighbor has built a shed with a sloping roof and the water is coming into our backyard and has nowhere to go. I research the issue and find that I can dig a French drain—basically, a pit holding a culvert that is covered with fine mesh and pea gravel, so the water can be stored and eventually be absorbed into the ground. I ask around and hire a man to dig the ditch. I say I'll pay him $50. He says he wants $50 per hour. I say that's too much and offer him $75 for the whole job. He mumbles something about later but shakes my hand.

I come back when it's done, and he says he wants $150: $50 per hour. I say that's not the agreement and pay him $75. He goes away angry.

About a week later, I notice that there are plants missing from the landscaping in our front yard. Just one here, one there, not enough to be noticeable. The man who had dug the ditch was a landscaper—in fact, the landscaper who had supplied the plants and had charged me hundreds of dollars to do it. While I couldn't prove it, the fact that the plants were expertly removed was pretty good evidence that he had come back and taken what he believed would make up what he perceived he had lost.

At first I was angry. I ranted and railed to my wife about it, and threatened to call the police, have him arrested for theft, or at least ruin his reputation. Then, I remembered the lawn-mowing incident.

In this incarnation, I was the bald, cigar-smoking tyrant who was gleeful that he had found someone to do a job for such a low price. The landscaper was me, only older. Yeah, he didn't handle it right, but he also felt the same feelings of being exploited. He had accepted the job because he had done work for me before and probably hoped for more work in the future. But I wasn't fair with him. I had offered him less than the job was worth, knowing that he had worked for me before and believing that he would not want to jeopardize possible work in the future. He accepted the lower price after voicing his misgivings, but rather than listen to him after the job was done and make it right, I had angrily rebuffed him.

Once I realized this, I laughed. Karma. I had passed on my youthful anger and shame in the same way the man whose lawn I had mowed had treated me, only this time, I was the creator of anger and shame.

Had I known recapitulation then—reviewing my actions objectively and releasing the emotions associated with them—perhaps I wouldn't have had to confront my own "mirror" in anger, embarrassment, and pain.

As it was, I waited a few weeks, had my wife call him to do some yardwork, and paid him handsomely. After a while, the missing plants reappeared. The cycle of resentment was broken.

FROM THE AUTHOR'S NOTEBOOK

BEING MY FATHER'S SON

I SEE A LOT OF MYSELF and my father in Pesavento's analogy of the Dark Mother. I don't mean my mother but the concept of divided loyalties. Like millions of others, my father came home from World War II victorious, having conquered the foreign foe. It was good versus evil, with the West allied against Nazi Germany. As Tom Brokaw wrote, his was the Greatest Generation.

His generation, through the GI Bill and postwar prosperity, also created a huge middle class that saw incomes and life chances rise. The men who came home from war refused to return to life on the farms where they had grown up; instead, they flocked to cities and created suburbia. They had the best standard of living ever known, and yet it wasn't enough to stop war, or competitiveness, or all the excesses of patriarchy.

Rather than winning a war and creating peace, they created another war, the Cold War, that made competitive greed over land, resources, and beliefs a matter of mutually assured destruction. Called MAD—and it truly was—this nuclear standoff meant that hundreds of millions of people lived in fear daily that one side would launch a missile strike that would end in the annihilation of both countries. Only now is it being revealed how close this came to happening during the Bay of Pigs, perhaps prevented only by a Russian submarine captain who refused to follow what turned out to be erroneous orders.[8]

To my young child's eyes, my father was a hero—and he was. He was a country boy who grew up on a farm in rural America, volunteered to go to war, and went through some of the bloodiest fighting in the Pacific. Stationed on Guam, he saw fellow soldiers picked off by snipers, waged constant guerilla warfare with a mobile, determined enemy, and lived off the land.

As a child, I played "war" with imaginary foxholes, shooting imaginary bullets, defeating imaginary enemies—often enough that my great, big, brave father one day took me aside and asked, "Jim, do you really want to do this?"

He explained to me the reality of war, the ugliness of it, how it turned men into killing machines, animals who lived by a credo of kill or be killed. There was nothing glamorous about it, he said. He volunteered for battle because he thought it was a way to fight for his country and be brave and valorous. But what he saw sickened him; he saw senseless slaughter, unimaginable atrocities, and fickle deaths that had no rhyme or reason. He saw his friends die and shared the survivors guilt with those who didn't catch the bullet that day.

I'm grateful to my father for giving me this talk. His words were heartfelt, and I could tell it was difficult for him to share, his words torn from his gut, not elegant but blunt, halting, and sincere. I remember it to this day, more than half a century ago.

Much of his anguish, as outlined in the introduction of this book, was played out in harsh and inappropriate ways. We have a generation of young men—veterans from Iraq, Afghanistan, and other conflicts around the globe—who are also carrying immeasurable pain and suffering. Certain shamanic practices, such as recapitulation, have helped me heal those wounds and not pass them along to my son and grandson. For example, when I was growing up, my parents were in their 20s and 30s. No wonder they made mistakes! Now I have been a parent, too, and have made my own mistakes.

It is true what the Bible says: When you were a child, you saw through the eyes of a child. Now, you can see the same events through the eyes of an adult, to grow with these experiences, put them in perspective, and move on.

Updating our memories through recapitulation, while practicing forgiveness, compassion, and gratitude, is a way toward inner growth and wisdom. It can help chart a path toward new beginnings unencumbered by unnecessary pain and resentment from the past.

My father's words had a profound effect on me. By sharing with me his pain and confusion, his own saga of manhood as a warrior, and explaining the facts of war versus the patriotic exhortation toward war and domination over others, I was able to see the truth that many of my generation had to learn the hard way. As a consequence of this sharing, from warrior to son, I chose a different way. I was a conscientious objector during the Vietnam War and pursued a path of peace, however elusive it sometimes seemed to be.

His were the words of an experienced adult, not the adolescent who urges toward events and outcomes he knows not. We need more such voices in our society, heeding the elders who have hard-won wisdom to share.

Review

Exploring life stages and relationships as definitions of manhood:

- There is no one definition of manhood; it changes over time.

- Our society has a historical narrative of men versus women dating back to before the Flood and Adam and Eve in the Bible with *The Epic of Gilgamesh*.

- Just as historical definitions of manhood are enduring, the definition of a man's selfhood as a man is impacted by important, enduring events, such as childhood, adolescence, and maturity.

- See how you define yourself, based on your history, role models, and significant life events. Are there areas you would like to redefine or explain to others? Practice the shamanic art of recapitulation to heal old wounds.

INTERNET KEY WORDS: *Epic of Gilgamesh, Enkidu, role model, warrior, peacemaker, goddess, wild man, dark mother, father wound, recapitulation*

Compounding the Problem—
Our Dysfunctional Society

Nature attains perfection but man never does…
the incurable unfinishedness keeps man perpetually immature,
perpetually capable of learning and growth.
— ERIC HOFFER, *REFLECTIONS ON THE HUMAN CONDITION*

In crafting a course or retreat on the subject of redefining the concept of manhood to fit emerging realities, the basic problem one
confronts is that our society is dysfunctional. So, however perfect a
new definition may be, it must exist in an imperfect system.

As we explored earlier, the dark mother, the absent father, skewed
and outdated archetypes, and the overall shift in gender roles—not
to mention the warped ideas of "male as superior" patriarchy that
have lingered into the modern age—raise a question. Is there any
hope for a balanced way to raise male children to become responsible, reasonable, rational adults? And where do you start?

Just as it's said that in the world of the blind, a one-eyed man is
king, it can also be said that visionaries are seen as eccentric oddballs
who don't fit in and must be banished. A child with emotional intel-
ligence beyond his years can be a blessing, but for that child it can
also be a curse in which he is subject to the taunts and the cruelties
for which children are famous. Indeed, adolescence may itself be seen
as the wail of differentiation, boosted by uncontrollable hormones.

What's a mother or father to do? Look for role models. But where
are the men?

Today, there are few channels for young men to learn how to become men. While the Boy Scouts of America is one avenue, it's not helped by its militaristic model (uniforms, hierarchy, salutes) or the fact that it historically has explicitly rejected gender diversity and failed to make significant inroads among minorities. Its primary tools of fieldcraft for self-reliance lack currency in a country increasingly urban and removed from its rural roots (however needed).

Churches have difficulty providing biblical role models because so much of the Old Testament is based on rigid role models that don't resonate with today's young people. Even the New Testament is problematic, because it teaches a form of leadership that modern American society, at least, absolutely rejects: a way of peace based on turning the other cheek; doing to others as you would have done to you; making personal sacrifices so that others might benefit; and choosing womblike love for all people regardless of circumstance rather than giving mercy, as by a victor or hierarchical ruler.

If everyone actually lived according to the New Testament, the world would be a much more considerate, compassionate, and loving place. Wouldn't it seem logical and rational for churches, or assemblages of people who gather for the sake of worship, divine inspiration, healing, and prayer, to respect the sacredness of men and women equally as spiritual beings lovingly put on this earth and provide role models for carrying that out? A look at early Christianity shows how that was originally taught but got derailed early on.

Equality of Men and Women Destroyed by Romans

It is now known that some of Jesus's teachings were carried forth in the three centuries after his death by the Gnostics, some of whom were disciples or relatives of Jesus, as revealed by the Nag Hammadi texts found in 1947. But the beliefs conflicted with many held by the authorities in Rome, hence "Gnostic," rather than being known as being "learned" (Greek *gnostikos*, from *gnōsis*, or knowledge) became associated with heresy.

The Gnostic texts are probably the clearest record of early Christianity. Until the Nag Hammadi texts were found few Gnostic documents remained, and the popular view of them was the one their conquerors promoted. So, through the centuries, the Gnostics have been frequently portrayed as a group of "heretics" promulgating dangerous and hateful ideas when, in fact, at the time, many of their ideas had great currency and legitimacy.

With the discovery of the Nag Hammadi texts, modern people can see for themselves what the Gnostics believed. In many ways, this find revealed more about the modern foundations of Christianity, beliefs coexistent with Judaism and influential in the writing of the Qur'an, than do the Dead Sea Scrolls.

When Constantine, the first Christian Roman emperor, made Paul's sect the only "official" Christian church in AD 313, there were three main branches of Christianity:

- The remnants of the Jewish Christian sect of Jesus's disciples
- The churches started by Paul
- The Gnostics

It is believed that the Gnostics evolved, in part, from the Essenes, and that John the Baptist, as well as Jesus and Simon Magus, the founder of Gnosticism, were all Essenes; indeed, it is reported that the earliest Jewish Christian followers of Jesus were called Essenes.

The Nag Hammadi texts reveal why the Paul faction so feared Gnostic ideas. First, the Gnostics did indeed have some major differences of belief with Paul's church, particularly whether the God of the Bible was the "true" God and whether a Supreme Being to

Jehovah existed. The Gnostics based that belief on the fact that if the devil tempted Jesus in the desert by offering him all the riches of the world, then that would mean the devil actually had the power to fulfill the offer, which would mean Jehovah was not omnipotent or truly a "supreme" being.

They also pointed to the words of Jehovah when speaking to Moses, that He was a "jealous" God and Moses should have no others before Him. They reasoned that if God were "jealous" there must be others; thus, he could not be supreme. The Gnostics also believed in reincarnation and astrology, and that souls rested in the houses of the constellations. The Dead Sea Scrolls pose similar theological musings.

In addition to these basic differences, the Gnostics had other ideas counter to Roman-backed Christianity that were more insidious. These ideas ran counter to the "official" church, which was intent on building power, aggressively amassing followers, and exercising strong central authority backed by government force:

- Like the Essenes, they believed that there was a divine spark in every human and each person could let that "light" be a guide to salvation.

- They did not believe that they needed a church or a church doctrine or "canon," as Paul's church demanded, to guide all believers. In fact, many Gnostics attended other churches, including Paul's, which seems to have angered his church's hierarchy even more; and they preferred meeting in each other's houses, negating the need for a church. It was a rather loose, individualistic confederation. The Essenes did not believe a temple or manmade structure of any kind held the spirit of the Creator. The absence of a physical building did not mean, however, that followers should be compelled to provide funds to support a hierarchy of priests, as with the Roman church.

- The Gnostics believed that they alone truly understood Christ's message, and that other branches had misinterpreted Jesus's mission and teachings. (The Essenes also believed that they alone had correctly interpreted the Creator's will, including their belief that a messiah, or anointed one, would appear.)

But, here is where modern-day Christianity may have been really short-changed (and Western civilization given a colossal detour) by the Roman-backed church:

- The Gnostics asserted that Jesus had male and female disciples, and that both were worthy of equal consideration. The Nag Hammadi identifies Gnostic-believing disciples as Philip, Matthew, Thomas, Bartholomew, and Mary Magdalene.

- They believed that women were equal to men in their communities without discrimination.

- And many of them believed that God—or what might more accurately be conceptualized as the Creator—was both male and female and had attributes of either, and both.

This "woman as coequal" approach in all things, from society to the divine, was a radical departure from the culture at the time.

Women had no rights under Jewish law. They could not, for example, be taught the Torah. They could not be witnesses in a court of law or initiate a divorce. They were little more than the property of their fathers or husbands. They could not go out in public without being escorted by a family member and had to be veiled in public. Men and women held separate public festivities, and if a woman was seen with men, say, at a dinner or banquet, it was assumed she was a prostitute.

So, for the Gnostics to reject this and confer equality on women in their churches was a serious offense in the eyes of the church of Paul. Even more offensive was the Gnostics' view of the Creator as female.

A text from the Nag Hammadi called *On the Origin of the World* expresses the Gnostic philosophy on the Creator, naming the Divine Force as Sophia, which is referred to as "Her." As the First Force or primal force, Sophia became "pregnant" of "Her" own accord and gave birth to matter, the first substance, water, "as with a woman giving birth to a child." The being that came forth was Yaldabaoth (Jehovah or Yahweh). Thus, all things, Jehovah, the angels, humans, Earth—everything—issued from the Womb of God, from the Goddess Sophia.[1]

You can imagine how well this went over with the likes of Paul, who it must be remembered was the author of such ideas as women should be silent in the presence of men and that women could not be teachers of men—much less, become pope. Those ideas were enshrined and were carried forward into Protestantism (Martin Luther equated girls with being weeds).[2]

Most early societies did view the earth as female and essential to life—all life. Without the male power, the seed, there would be no life, but without the womb there could be no life. Hence, they were different but equal; one had no primacy over the other. In most early societies, such as that of the Essenes, the co-creator quality of Earthly Mother and Heavenly Father was accepted without question worldwide.

Our Religions Are Basically Flawed

So how did it come about that in Christianity, the Father begat the Son with only a relatively minor female character who seems to have little say or influence in the matter?

Roman emperor Constantine assembled the Council of Nicaea in AD 325, and bending to Constantine's wishes, approved a creed essentially making the godhead of God and the Son, Jesus, equal with the Holy Ghost. At that assemblage—which, of course, was all male—the godhead of the church was established. Determining that Jesus is a part of God and thus not "created" made Jesus coequal with God and separate from humanity; it also forever altered the idea that the Creator could be dual, as with an Earthly Mother and Fatherly Spirit. Those who didn't agree were immediately exiled.

Taking advantage of the gathering, Constantine began a campaign to determine the order and organization of the church. He ordered 50 copies of a bible, or collection of sacred writings he authorized, to be supplied to churches he ordered to be built. He thereby officially put the emperor's stamp of approval on this church and its teachings, saying that all Christian churches must regard it as "indicative of the Divine will."

The Roman emperor then signed orders that anyone who didn't agree with the council's decision would be banished or put to death. Immediately, other groups that did not agree with the official church found themselves persecuted, as they had been before Christianity was the official Roman church; their churches were confiscated, their possessions seized, and their books burned.

With this act, the belief that God has a female aspect was discarded and all references to that principle destroyed and believers persecuted. It was heresy, and not to be condoned. With it was banished the idea that angels are coexistent in the ceremonies of the church, and the time-honored agricultural feasts and festivals were stripped from holy writ.

All references to women as in any way coequal to men were removed. That included the Infancy Gospel of Christ, the story of Jesus's upbringing, in which Christ's mother Mary is seen as a strong female role model, and the Gospel of Mary, in which Mary Magdalene disputes views by her fellow disciples defining her authority to teach. (It's surmised by many scholars today that Jesus and Mary Magdalene were married and that the wedding feast where Jesus turned water into wine was at his own wedding.)

Also dismissed and destroyed by the official patriarchal Christianity were competing beliefs about the nature of the divine and its origins that reached back thousands of years. This included Persian and Ancient Egyptian beliefs found in the Gnostic texts that portrayed the Creator as female. (Among them was one of the oldest extant records of a female divinity, a goddess text in Greek entitled *The Thunder: Perfect Mind*, possibly stemming back to Isis worship.) Extinguished was diversity of thought and intellectual freedom of expression, discussion, and resolution as a democratic way of finding truth, as the Gnostics extolled—divine revelation was literally the guiding light.[3]

The notion that women in the church were equal was officially silenced. Having relations with women was now considered unclean, and celibacy was deemed a more spiritual way of being, uncontaminated by the evil of women. The voices of women in the Church as authorities and teachers equal to men were silenced for millennia, a legacy that is only slowly crumbling today. Indeed, young people might find spiritual guidance more alluring if churches resurrected some of the chapters that gave examples of female leadership that were cut out of the early bibles by the Romans.

Traditional Archetypes Fail to Guide Young Men

Where are the roles that young men today can adopt to meet modern needs and expectations and offer spiritual guidance? The roles assigned by society—that is, the ones that provide Gilgamesh's paycheck—don't value self-sacrifice and giving unto others. These essential traits were found in Native America and, indeed, among indigenous people around the globe before modern nation-states emerged based on the Roman dominator model.

We cannot go back to Enkidu. The tassels of his corn hair have been shorn (or genetically modified), and he has succumbed to the comely delights of iTunes and smartphones. Our traditional archetypes are skewed and wrong for today.

By definition, the word "archetype" means the original pattern or model from which all things of the same kind derive. In Jungian psychology, the concept of archetype is extended to include the inherited "collective unconscious" idea, a pattern of thought or imagery that is present in all individuals. It's a pernicious concept. We adhere to an idea or image of something, and by doing so we promote that concept or image. Archetypes are both *overt* (that is, promoted consciously and held up as examples to be emulated) and *covert* (that is, guiding our thoughts and behavior subconsciously as guides and prejudices).

An example would be an advertisement in which someone goes to the pharmacy to make a purchase after reading an advertisement for a certain product. The pharmacist sees the purchase and reaffirms the customer's choice, saying it is a good one based on sound science and praising the customer for buying it with positive phrases such as

"You have good taste" or "You certainly know your products. That's an excellent choice."

In this case, the advertiser chooses an actor who looks like the target audience or who that target audience aspires to be (men or women with disposable income between the ages of 18 and 34). The actor displays the behavior the advertiser wants (buy the product), then the message is reinforced by an authority figure who is depicted praising the behavior of the customer. All this in 30 seconds.

That's how archetypes are built and reinforced in our society. We see and model behavior presented to us as authoritative or worth emulating. As the saying goes, the tree grows as the tree is bent. Accept certain archetypes while young, and they become laws in our minds that govern our thoughts and actions; eventually, they become part of us.

Where are our major models for behavior found today? Sports is one avenue. For men, sports offers a unique blend of aggression and rules, team cohesion, and individual achievement (heroism). Women in our society often seem baffled by the fanaticism (the origin of the term sports "fan") among men for team sports. While participation in sports in the lower schools is a common channel for higher levels of team play, as part of the physical education curriculum, relatively few male children achieve high levels of proficiency in team sports. So why the attachment?

Among men generally, even without professional sports teams in their geographic area, affiliation with a team offers a sense of belonging to a group and an avenue for self-identification larger than individual pursuits. This sense of belonging to a community while simultaneously upholding the values of competition, winning, and heroism acts as a bonding mechanism among men. Studies show that this identification is further strengthened by increased geographic mobility in today's world and the decline of traditional social and community ties. Following professional sports provides a buffer from feelings of alienation and depression, while giving a sense of belonging and self-worth. As an icebreaker in social situations, it offers an avenue for inclusion and the building of social ties, while also within social groups allowing maintenance of standing within the group.[4]

This individual bonding and social identification mechanism, along with cohesive characteristics for a social system as a whole, has been around in various forms around the globe. In Native American societies, for example, ball games created a similar bonding mechanism—and it was taken even more seriously by its players and fans than American football and European soccer today.

In Mesoamerican societies, such as the Maya, it was the *winning* team on the ball court that had the honor of being sacrificed to live with the gods, and players' beating hearts were cut out of their chests and held aloft for the crowd to see. In the Southeastern United States, tribes would decide territorial boundaries and other important conflicts through stickball games rather than going to war. The religious significance of sports was represented in virtually all American tribes through the antics of the Thunder Twins or similar gods who played a stickball game with the earth as their ball in a continuing battle between good and evil. This was contextual, not absolute: Neither of the twins was "bad"; they were immortal and beyond the understanding of human beings, but the consequences of their game had profound effects upon the world.

If sports had more of a spiritual aspect (which many sports leaders try to make it with prayers for victory, and so forth), it might serve a greater function as a balanced role model for men. However, the status of sports in general, and professional sports in particular, is riddled with misogyny. As Michael A. Messner of the University of Southern California has noted, organized sports have come to serve as a primary institutional means for bolstering the faltering ideology of male superiority. The development of female athleticism represents a genuine quest by women for equality, control of their own bodies, and self-definition, he notes, and as such represents a challenge to the ideological basis of male domination.[5]

If you doubt that there are ideological gender roles in sports, ask yourself: Would you want your daughter to be a lineman in the National Football League? Or a cheerleader? Is the well-publicized calling each other "wusses" or worse as goads and criticisms a positive role model for young men? Can a person participate in team sports without gender bashing, or worse?

As this book was being written, the American sports world was awash in yet another controversy involving violence against women, with a top athlete caught on video punching his fiancee (now his wife) and dragging her out of an elevator. This seeming straw that broke the camel's back regarding violent attitudes by athletes toward women prompted well-known CBS sports anchor James Brown to lament: "This is yet another call for men to stand up to take responsibility for their thoughts, their words, their deeds. Our silence is deafening and deadly." And, as if seeing the need even for a book like this one, he called for "ongoing, comprehensive education of men of what healthy manhood is all about."[6]

But rather than embracing the changes underway toward greater equality and respect in male and female relations, many men are railing against them. This is particularly true in talk radio and sports. As Michael Kimmel points out, the title of basketball player Mariah Burton Nelson's book is *The Stronger Women Get, the More Men Love Football.*[7] Women, minorities, and immigrants are all blameworthy for the plight of the poor white male in talk radio, which blames the "feminazis" for everything.

You can't blame this negative male behavior on testosterone. Carefully controlled studies of increasingly elevated testosterone levels in young men have shown only mild effects in aggression, sexual or otherwise.[8] However, it is true that libido, or sex drive, is driven by testosterone levels in both sexes. Biochemically driven behavior—or thinking between your legs—is a unisex activity; it is just more socially pronounced among men.[9]

Archetypes Fail

Leaders in the field of male empowerment have sought to define the individual boy-into-man journey on the basis of existential archetypes, defined as King, Warrior, Magician, and Lover. Authors Robert Moore and Douglas Gillette, in their book *King, Warrior, Magician, Lover: Rediscovering the Archetypes of the Mature Masculine,* define the modern male based on what they term "psychological facts." King energy is primal in all men, they write, and underlies and includes the three other qualities. Such a man displays selflessness, wisdom like Solomon, and approximates God in his majesty, the primal father, Adam. In his maturity, such a man is, they say, the good Warrior, a positive Magician, and a great Lover.

Each of these qualities is seen as important to defining manhood, providing archetypes for behavior. As Sam Keen, author of *Fire in the Belly: On Being A Man*, puts it: War, work, and sex form the triad of male initiation rites and the pillars of male identity.

While these archetypes may exemplify some aspects of manhood, they are terribly dated and not very useful in our changing society. To be blunt, it's a very Greek way of looking at the world—the same ancient society that objectified women. It's painful to read the examples of children outlined in such books as successful boy children/men and unsuccessful ones who don't "measure up" to the macho version of manhood presented. The criteria in such books simply mimic the dysfunctions of historical dominator philosophy, putting the onus on men to simply grow into the archetypes the authors present—essentially asking them to, as Facebook CEO Sheryl Sandberg asked women to do, "lean in," to persevere.

Why create failure as a result of our inability to live up to others' expectations? Rather than creating role models, archetypes, and tools for men to grow into their spiritual selves as balanced and complete human beings, such books ask men to forfeit their individually and accept beliefs and modes of behavior they might not believe or feel comfortable performing. This is a backwards way of looking at life and the role of human beings—all human beings, in all their diversity—in society. Both women and men are living down to their lowest potential in acquiescing to narrow, restrictive definitions of acceptable belief and behavior, not rising up by seeing their shared potential as new and unique individuals in a new and exciting world.

Why Perpetuate the Warrior Myth?

Certainly, in times of war, a warrior is needed. But war is a finite condition, not a way of being. Even the consummate Yaqui shaman Don Juan Matus taught that labeling one's persona only got in the way of personal power. So when he exhorted Peruvian-American author Carlos Castañeda, his apprentice, to "be a warrior," he wasn't saying to become and stay a warrior; he was saying to be a warrior in cutting off attachments, including self-concepts and limiting beliefs. "Make your inventory and then throw it away," he said.

Only when we laugh at our concepts of who we are—or, as one of my Lakota medicine man teachers stressed again and again, "Who you *think* you are"—can you become who you really are!

This celebration and promotion of warrior status is understandable, given the fact that the United States and much of the world has been in a state of unending war ("terrorism") for more than a decade. Indeed, there are young men entering draft age who have never consciously known peacetime. This war is undeclared, but the fact that Congress allows our own country to spy on us and remove civil liberties under the Orwellian-named Patriot Act ensures it will go on and on, perhaps forever. It's especially telling that this war is with an unseen, unknown, and unconquerable enemy; our own military actions seem to perpetuate it by creating more terrorists. That ought to say something both about the actual cause of and need for such a war.

Native American tribes determined centuries ago that warrior status should be limited, as should war. When the first Europeans came, they found that men who had been off to war were not allowed back into the villages until they had been cleansed. This was not just a physical washing; it could last for days or weeks, with sweat lodges set up so that the warriors could be cleared of negative energy. Returning warriors were put on fasts and underwent rituals designed to rid them of the demons of war and return them to a state of peace.

Only after the holy men of the tribe were certain that the warriors were back in their true selves, showing their "true face," not the "false face" of war, were they allowed to enter the village, in order to resume their normal lives of being husbands, fathers, uncles, and sons.

We know from a decade of war in America—and particularly those in the National Guard, who were snatched from their homes for overseas deployment, then unceremoniously mustered in and out for subsequent tours—that soldiers who are put on combat duty without proper psychological training, or mustered out without great care, have difficulty readjusting to civilian life.

In addition to the staggering number of young men maimed by roadside bombs in Iraq and Afghanistan or suffering the lasting effects of concussions, the number of returned soldiers with post-traumatic stress disorder (PTSD) is a clear warning that a constant state of war is not healthy for a society or the individual, and our culture as it exists is ill-equipped to help these men adjust. In light of this, do we really want to continue to promote the warrior archetype as a desirable state of manhood?

The Dead Hand of Archetypes

The problem with looking at archetypes as a way of defining manhood is that they are, at heart, dead—and dysfunctional. They are dead because they prescribe behaviors that happened in the past. While an historical narrative can be a good guide for current and future events, it is becoming increasingly clear that the old narratives in our society aren't working and, in fact, are often toxic holdovers from grim times.

For example, let's look at the King archetype. If fairy tales are our guide—and how else are we supposed to learn about kingliness, since monarchies have largely been ceremonial in modern societies for the past 200 years or so?—then kingship is conferred by birth, not earned. In other words, one is born to it. If you are not born a king, you're just out of luck, kiddo. As far as hierarchy goes, it's a closed society, the elite of elites. There is no democracy to it or pro-motions through merit (unless through force of arms, you conquer and behead the current occupant of the throne).

What could be better than a king? Hmmm. Well, a queen, per-haps? Except how does one become a queen? In Sleeping Beauty, probably one of the most well-known fairy tale plots, a woman can become queen by essentially being dead—inert, that is, until a handsome prince walks by. What does this say about upward mobility or self-determination for women? And of princes? That young men will kiss a corpse in deserted woods if it's female, not badly decomposed, and nobody is looking?

Seriously, the archetypes are not all that inspiring. But, even here, the reality these days is far different. Princesses now become rulers in their own right. The governments of Europe have been leading the charge in changing the rules of succession so that daughters can become "king"—even over the objections of their own fathers. For example, Victoria, Crown Princess of Sweden, was made crown princess and heir apparent instead of her younger brother after a 1979 act of parliament changed succession to the throne so that a monarch's eldest child could rule without regard to gender. Her father, King Carl XVI Gustaf, opposed the change. Obviously, archetypes, fairy tales, and old notions of kinghood haven't kept up with the changes underway in society.

For more about the deleterious effect of old fairy tales on women's aspirations and self-definition, see the book *Spinning Straw Into Gold: What Fairy Tales Reveal about the Transformations in a Woman's Life* by Joan Gold. (In fact, those interested in determining deleterious effects on men's aspirations and self-definitions should also read the book, as it lists the odd traits that supposedly make up men's roles.)

While in days of yore, Mom may have read the books aloud to children perched in her lap, the little ears hearing the stories were male and female and both were making assumptions about role behaviors. While fear and jealousy are the messages to girls (as mother or daughter) in the tale of *Beauty and The Beast*, the messages to young men are that sex is brutish and ugly and as a man he should expect total obedience, especially among daughters, and even a tinge of incest. Talk about dysfunction!

And why did Sleeping Beauty sleep? What was so frightening in her inner self that she would shut down and go dormant for years? Somewhere across America, there are little girls grown into women who are secretly waiting for their prince to come—sleeping, not acting; wishing, not directing their lives; and suffering because they have internalized this archetype.

And guess what? There are young men across America who are going through life without love and happiness because they have no clue that there is a beautiful maiden next door pining away in her self-imposed slumber, all because she has swallowed the ideal that women don't take charge of their lives and honestly express their wants and needs.

And what of Eve, Pandora, and Psyche? As fairy tales would have it, each of these females is disobedient, the bringer of trouble, and responsible for the ills of humankind, while their male counterparts are wise and knowledgeable, not reckless and irresponsible like these women. But turn it around, and what does it really say about men? That for all their pretensions, they are outwitted by women? That men know they will be disobeyed and live in denial? That man was meant to be the constant unwitting dupe?

Remember, Enkidu sat at the feet of the harlot to learn about the world. And it was only through Gilgamesh's eyes that the woman was a harlot. In her temple, she was a keeper of secrets, a confidante of the goddess, and knew how to bend men to her will. Only Gilgamesh's physical power could trump the spiritual power of the woman and, even then, she delighted in her role as temptress and teacher, shameless in her wanton desire for the untamed man, unbound by the labels put upon her by the men who were her oppressors.

Sexual Oppression in the Form of Repression

Being an "oppressor" or a "dominator" is a strong word for men to accept, and it's true that individual men may wonder, how can that be? How could anyone see me as an oppressor or in any way dominating? I have problems finding my car keys in the morning, and my wife pretty much dictates what I do!

The ways of liberation and oppression are wily, often obscure, and rear up in strange and wondrous ways—not obvious at all, except perhaps in hindsight.

Modern young men think nothing of their wives or girlfriends having a vibrator, and even joining in the fun with it; however, it's truly a liberating tool that, along with the birth control pill, changed the course of male/female sexuality—a shift that your great-grandmother might still find shocking and your great-grandfather immoral. The distance that women have traveled toward sexual liberation in less than 100 years is astounding. Despite the preceding 2,000 years of sexual oppression, this represents a return of sorts, since goddess cultures allowed women free sexual expression as a sacred act.

When it comes to sex, the past is not only the future; there is rapid evolution in the present, too. For example, in your great-grandmother's time, a popular belief was that women weren't supposed to feel sexual arousal—it was actually considered a disease and even a chronic condition.[10] Until the 1920s, the treatment of sexually unsatisfied women was for a physician or midwife to manually stimulate the genitalia so the "afflicted woman can be aroused to paroxysm" and thereby relieve the symptoms of distress. Descriptions of the "disease" go back to the Hippocratic corpus, the works of Celsus in the first century AD, and continued virtually unchanged into the 20th century. Astoundingly, this "affliction" of "hysteria," or simply having a libido, what some might call horniness or desire for orgasm, was listed as a disease until the American Psychiatric Association dropped the term in 1952.

The invention of the portable, battery-operated vibrator in the late 1960s was a liberating tool for many women. Enough so that today, in locker rooms and other venues where "macho" males may hang out, it's widely cursed as a substitute for men. They might be partly right: it *is* a substitute for some men—those who subordinate women or treat them as sex objects and not partners.

The sociological literature, however, does not support the view that women have rejected men sexually following the introduction of the vibrator. Women continue to enjoy loving relationships with men, but now have the option to share lovemaking beyond relieving either partner's "hysteria." Vibrators and other devices, oils, and creams can enhance the sexual experience of both partners. It should be remembered that sexual male penetration, while it may be enjoyable in itself, is only one facet of lovemaking. It's estimated that greater than 50 percent (some sources say 70 percent) of women report that male sexual penetration alone does not bring orgasm. Sexual liberation is a two-way street, with men and women today being allowed more freedom to share intimacy in various ways for mutual satisfaction.

The Kingship archetype, involving a male having power and control over a woman, only perpetuates dominator behaviors, including sexual aggression. It denies the possibility of men and women sharing all facets of life as equals. The fallacy of the male dominator lover archetype is that it promotes the belief that women will accept a return to male-female relationships of an earlier era—a time when the sexual satisfaction of women was considered a disease, an unnatural state; when women existed solely to satisfy the king and produce heirs to the throne; when women were viewed as objects and allowed neither complaint nor pleasure.

Mothers, do you want your sons to be part of this outdated Kingship narrative? Do you want them to be oppressors or victims of their own folly? Fathers, do you not see that by accepting the old fairy tales of obedience, war, and male expectations of what constitutes a leader and lover men are merely cuckolding themselves? In so doing, they are forcing the positive and shared attributes of male and female into the shadows, where they emerge as tricks and grief, shame and betrayal. It is a dysfunctional tale we weave for our children to follow, with their eyes focused not on their unlimited potential but on failings associated with their gender.

The women's movement has made a good case that the fairy tales that informed and shaped young girls of a generation ago created dysfunctional lives and unrealistic, even self-sabotaging expectations. Lacking is a similar wake-up call for young men that their roles in the growing-up stories are equally dysfunctional; they lead to false self-identities and behaviors that not only are rejected by women and society but ought to be rejected by men.

Sex is a normal physical and emotional function of human life that transcends childbirth. Among primates, humans are the only ones that have sexual desire and functioning independent of the reproductive cycle. Men and women can have active, healthy, fulfilling sex lives their entire lives. Research among subjects ranging in age from 18 to 102 has shown that people who regularly engage in sex look younger than their chronological age and also enjoy better health and weight control.[11]

In energy medicine, sexual functioning revolves around the first three chakras. Unfortunately, the very scientific names for the female human anatomy in some cases reflect guilt and shame over female sexuality, since they were given by the patriarchal system. The major nerve to the vulva is called the pudendal nerve, the Latin root word of *pudenda* meaning "shame." Men can help women alleviate negativity stored in this area of the body through gentle stimulation and holding in a loving, sharing way.[12]

While modern medicine in the form of Viagra and other medications and devices can help men with erectile dysfunction associated with aging, it shouldn't be lost on men that nature takes care of its own. While older men may be slower to develop erections, and those may be less stiff than when they were younger, they also presumably are having intercourse with older women who are slower to be receptive and may be using additional lubricants. Also, nature in its wisdom allows the expansion of the vagina during and after childbirth, so that men with less erect penises may find penetration easier as they and their partners age. The penchant of younger women to "take an extra stitch" in repairing the vagina after childbirth so that their partners might have a tighter fit (sometimes even more than before birth) can be a disadvantage for older male partners.

Men should applaud sexual equality as a means of achieving greater intimacy, sharing, and personal growth. In order for this to happen, and for sexual dysfunction to be dissolved, men and women should be honest about their bodies, their upbringing, the baggage they bring into a relationship, and seek to help heal each other through their love. Both men and women can release past trauma through openness and pursuing energy medicine techniques that also are gaining traction in today's world. [13]

Applying a holistic approach to relationships—physical, mental, spiritual—takes intimacy away from shame-based views of the world associated with paternalism and patriarchy and restores it to a celebration of life. In such a milieu, feelings of equality and mutual self-respect are carried forward. Indeed, the ongoing sexual liberation of men and women, in all their diversity, is a key element in the forces propelling change. As it's said, we are all spiritual beings in physical bodies. We share far more than that which divides us, and our diversity is our strength, creating joy if we will only grasp it, embrace it, live it!

Men and Women in a Historical Box

Men can look at female archetypes as expressed in fairy tales and so forth and see what women are rejecting and, by extension, how men's models are no longer functioning; however, both men and women are in the same boat when it comes to what to do or how to survive the changing roles of men and women. Both are caught in a historical box, making it inevitable that male and female roles should level out, dating back to the years prior to the American Revolution.

While the American Revolution helped advance the cause of class equality and liberation from aristocratic rule, it really was primarily a fight among men about manhood. Indeed, while the American Revolution unleashed the genie of democratization upon the world, a benefit for all humans, it also reinvigorated patrimony and male domination in the Americas.

As R.W. Connell outlines in his book *Masculinities*, the modern gender order came into being in Europe between AD 1450 and AD 1650 (the "long 16th century," as French historian Fernand Braudel called it). During that period four configurations of "masculinity" took shape:

- The introduction of the conjugal household, or "married monk," on the order of Martin Luther, replaced monastic sexual denial with compulsory heterosexuality as the most honored form of sexuality. It exalted the concept of the individual right to have a direct relationship with God.

- The creation of overseas empires where men were allowed to conquer whole Native societies through war, rape, and pillage occurred. Natives were subjugated in the name of God and conquest, without any consideration for human rights or dignity, or even legal order, other than free license. As a result, slavery and warfare as natural states of being under a system of male military domination were implemented (even the imperial states headed by women were unable to contain the violence).

- The growth of cities that promoted capitalism and wealth generation took place. With it came the hardening of gender differences in jobs, roles, duties, even physiology and fashion. This tied the concept of wealth to Protestant ideology, which stated that those who acquired wealth were preordained to do so and hence smiled upon by God, justifying gender and class subordination (class warfare).

- The consolidation of patriarchy in all areas of life, including religion. This led to the persecution of Quakers, who treated men and women equally, and was a factor in the English Civil War, during which the state publicly proclaimed women as equal. The persecution of equal rights led to the strong centralized state.

The birth of the American Revolution itself was a rejection by American men of their subservient state under British colonial rule, while simultaneously reimposing it on their own terms in the Americas.

As Michael Kimmel outlines in *Manhood in America: A Cultural History*, the American Revolution was steeped in worries over manliness. The term manhood was synonymous with adulthood; just as black slaves were called "boys," white colonists, as sons of tyranny, felt enslaved by the despotic English father. The Declaration of Independence was a declaration of manly adulthood. In a letter to Thomas Jefferson, fellow founding father John Adams worried about the seeming inevitable trend toward a more prosperous society and a less manly citizenry, asking, "Will you tell me how to prevent luxury from producing effeminacy…?"

The rise of the "New Man," a self-made man of the frontier—as opposed to the effeminacy of the aristocracy—was a powerful theme of the time. Those ideas have continued to be a theme in American politics to the present day, with former President George W. Bush proclaiming himself a "war leader," even as he artfully dodged the draft during the Vietnam War, and portraying his opponent John Kerry, a genuine Purple Heart recipient during that war, as effeminate and cowardly. (Bush's father, who Bush seemed compelled to outdo by invading Iraq, had to fight the image of being an effeminate blue blood, promoting in his campaign that he was "a fighter, not a wimp.") War and violence have been equated with patriarchy and manliness in America since its founding.

White men of the time defined their manliness and worth by the number of their possessions, which were protected by the laws they imposed and by violence; the definition of equality (and the right to vote) therefore only extended to white men over the age of 21 who possessed property. Women, slaves, and land, were assumed to be part of the package of being considered a true man in Revolutionary Era America. This continued to be the case through to the beginnings of the Industrial Era in the mid-19th century, the onset of the American Civil War (when slavery was only practiced in the South), and afterward, when men started to become "wage slaves."

Women may have invented agriculture, but close behind that

achievement, men invented slavery—and the earliest slaves were women. As Gerda Lerner notes in *The Creation of Patriarchy*, settled societies linked to the surplus of food produced by agriculture made slavery a winning proposition. But men as slaves didn't work out too well. A copper hoe is not much different than a copper hatchet in the hands of a male warrior: it took too many overseers to ensure that copper hoes were kept digging in the ground. Women made better slaves because they often bore children (a perk for the male slave owners, who achieved sexual gratification through rape). Women were kept in line though fear over treatment of their offspring and their hopes that their children's lives might be better. Under this system, conquered men were simply killed, while women found "value" as slaves.

Slavery quickly became an important part of settled civilization, Lerner writes. It added to economic organization and forced labor (wealth building), which led to the development of ancient civilization. Hence, the invention of slavery became a "crucial watershed for humanity."

Slavery also depends on ways to distinguish slave from slave owner. In the case of women, women's sexuality and reproductive potential became a commodity to be exchanged or acquired. This led to the practice of enslaving women to build harems as a means of displaying wealth in patriarchal societies, and of counting lineage purely through male lines. While men "belonged in" a household or lineage, women "belonged to" a male who had inherited or acquired rights within those lineages. Women became marginal, not considered fully human in the realm of human rights, just as African slaves and others lost their human rights by becoming marginalized. [14]

The repercussions of women in Western society not being treated equally through history—indeed, little more than a form of chattel, or slave—has ramifications that continue to the present day, even as the vestiges of it are being addressed in law and custom. The residual effects of this underlying belief system add immeasurably to the dislocations in men's beliefs about themselves and what constitutes manhood today.

Even in the 20th century, women weren't considered fully independent human beings. During the Great Depression of the 1930s, author Norman Cousins noted that the number of unemployed men was about 10 million, the same as the number of women in the workplace. He suggested that women "who shouldn't be working anyway" simply be fired and men be hired, adding, "Presto! No unemployment… No Depression!"

The Depression had a lasting effect on the definition of manhood that exists today. It forced many men to abandon their faith in their jobs and their work as a definition of manliness. Manhood had to be redefined to specific traits, behaviors, and attitudes. Something had to take the place of the workplace as men's proving ground. It quickly became war.

World War II defined the "manliness" of a generation of men, even as their Baby Boomer sons bore the brunt of the expectations and obligations resulting from it, and rejected those notions in the 1960s and '70s. But war remains a proving ground among young men with today's unending warfare.

It should be noted here that even in Native society, warfare was considered an honorable definition of manhood. Before the Revolutionary War, when the British were trying to keep sufficient Native American allies to offset the French claims to North America, Cherokee and Iroquois chiefs were brought together in an attempt to broker a peace between them. For generations, their young men had made the several days' travel back and forth to "count coup" and steal from one another to show their bravery, occasionally resulting in death. Both sides reacted with horror to the British idea of ending the practice, asking how could they contain and focus the energies of their young men and find honorable ways for them to prove their manhood? This, however, was merely skirmishing, maintaining boundaries, not the all-out war we have today.

The tide of equality, however, continues to roll in. The three great Western imperatives of the last 300 years are Christianity, democracy, and capitalism. Each has within it the need for equality, however limiting may be the rules or constructs that are imposed upon it.

Consider:

CHRISTIANITY: As noted earlier, Jesus didn't say suffer the little male children to come unto me, but all children—all races, creeds, genders. Many early Christians, like the Jewish Essenes before them, of which Jesus may have been affiliated, recognized male and female as equal in discipleship and leadership as keepers of divine wisdom. Women were considered persons in their own right, as were men, which was considered a dangerous idea to both the mainstream Hebrew and Roman power structures of the time.[15]

Both men and women were educated in Rome during Jesus's time. It wasn't until the year AD 200 that the Letter of Timothy was endorsed by the male-dominated Pauline sects of Christianity proclaiming that women should "learn in silence with all submissiveness" and asserting that the Church should "permit no woman to teach or have authority over men."

Prior to this proclamation, Christian enclaves lived according to *agape*, or brotherly and sisterly love. As discussed earlier, by the time of the Council of Nicea, convened by Roman emperor Constantine in AD 325, all references to women as coequal to men were stripped from holy writ, silencing the female voice in the compendium that became our modern Bible.

The history of the Church and the Bible is not a happy one for women. The original works in the Bible that were inclusive of women and considered holy were removed. And then there was the horrendous behavior that characterized Christian zealotry, as reflected in the persecution associated with the Inquisition and other barbarities. These can only be called male attributes gone amok and have skewed modern understandings of the Christian message.

The Good News, as filtered through a "boy's only" sign, does not resonate either with new converts or with women with a heart and hands willing to aid the world, as Jesus would have done. Established churches will either have to accept this fact or continue to suffer declines in leadership and numbers. Indeed, they should champion the original words and deeds of the religion that bears Christ's name.

DEMOCRACY: With the origins of the American democratic movement, the battle cry that all men are created equal has stood as both an ideal and a challenge—that all human beings, regardless of gender, racial origin, or creed, should be treated equally with the same inalienable rights.

The late Reverend Martin Luther King Jr. understood all too well that the idea that democratic freedoms and individual liberty could only be afforded white males had long outgrown its limitations; not only that, it made the very idea of freedom a ludicrous farce without universal application to men and women of all races and creeds. Today, King's view that "the sons of the slaves and slave owners would one day sit down and break bread together" seems antiquated, in a time when black entrepreneurs, CEOs, even the President of the United States of America reach the highest rungs of society.

Implicit but not stated in King's message is that the *daughters* of slaves and slave owners should also break bread together. Again, the imperative of democratization is pushing more equality to the forefront, and it makes sense.

When Thomas Hobbes wrote in 1651 that "one man cannot… claim to himself any benefit to which another may not pretend as well," it's apparent that the meaning applies to all humankind without discrimination of any sort. So, too, in 1762, when Jean-Jacques Rousseau wrote in *The Social Contract or Principles of Political Right* that all men are born free and equal but "he is everywhere in chains," it's hard to imagine today that he meant white males should walk free while women of all colors by rights should remain behind in bondage.

The devil in democracy, which Dr. King rightly pointed out, is that equality means equality, individual freedom applies to individuals, and democratic principles mean nothing unless they are equally applied. To accept other terms, or limit them, is the very essence of tyranny. That imperative, which in many and fitful ways has erupted in places as diverse as the Bastille in France and Colonial America, and more recently in the presidential palace in Egypt and in Tiananmen Square in China, continues around the world today and shows no indication of slowing.

CAPITALISM: Modern corporate capitalism may have its roots in the buccaneers of old, who were entitled by governments to raid, pillage, and destroy, and in the trading companies that were given monopolies over indigenous peoples and settlers to the advantage of the privileged class. But it is also a movement unto itself. Under corporate capitalism, the dollar is king and all else—love, compassion, kindness, even people—is secondary at best. In its ruthless pursuit of profit, it also is a great leveler and exalter on its own terms.

Prior to Adam Smith, the 18th-century Scottish political economist, governments were seen to be divinely inspired and subject to the whims of monarchs who owed their primacy to feudal allegiances. But Smith's 1776 *Wealth of Nations* turned the world upside down. It asserted that the basis of freedom is prosperity, and that the "hidden hand" of the free market is a more perfect ruler, allowing individuals the liberty to pursue their own interests and be rewarded for it.

Smith's view may have had its roots in the Protestant movement, which ordained that God took an interest in those who were living according to His precepts and rewarded them through Providence in Heaven and on Earth. But it also reaffirmed the principle that men (let us read: humankind) were free to adopt their own relations and have their own interpretations of God's Word and the world around them, not be subject to the edicts of a pope or a king.

Of course, one can't set one's own course without the principle of private property—meaning property that is owned by the free individual as opposed to the king or aristocracy. So, individual liberty, religious freedom, the sanctity of private property, and the inalienable rights of men (freedom, equality, human rights) all became wrapped up into one big ball in the American Revolution that same year.

The point I am trying to make is that this impetus is still strong today. It may well be that our current democratic systems are being throttled by chokeholds artfully inserted to prevent the rabble (male and female) from storming the Bastille and throwing the rascally One Percenters of Occupy Wall Street fame out on their well-fed arses. But Smith's "hidden hand" is still pushing men and women today into new situations of equality and freedom, as defined by its narrow economic view on life, and that has far-reaching implications.

It matters not one whit if one holds a patriarchal view that men should be paid more than women if the most highly qualified job candidates at the best price (salary level) are women. Increasingly, that is the case. Again, the historical impetus is toward more democratization, less male hegemony. Modern corporations and businesses are having to adjust, as are men and women in our society.

We are entering an age of "excarnation," one where we are the makers of who we become.[16] Incarnation is "Word made flesh," as Christian theology teaches, but in a world where all the knowledge of the ages is at our fingertips, we are each—male and female—able to remake our images and, hence, our "selves," as we experience and perceive the world without outside pressure or normative controls, such as archetypes.

We are no longer bound by gender roles enforced by dated concepts, or by outworn traditions or constructs that served in industrial and preindustrial societies. This is the society that is now emerging, as the trends in jobs, lifestyles, and familial realities attest. At present, couples, families, and individuals—both male and female—know that their lives, relationships, work, leisure, even how they define themselves are all changing. In 1960s rock group Buffalo Springfield's immortal words, "There's something happening here. But what it is ain't exactly clear… "

What we are witnessing, each one of us, is the end of an old order and the beginning of a new. According to three-time Pulitzer Prize–winning *New York Times* columnist Thomas L. Friedman, the world is evolving out of "freedom from" dictators, conventions, even archetypes, into "freedom to" live your life, speak your mind, and be yourself regardless of sexual, religious, or political orientation.[17]

The great engine toward equality cannot, and will not, be denied, even if it is a messy and uncertain affair, seemingly three steps forward and two steps back. We see that with the Arab Spring, Tiananmen Square, and other faltering steps around the globe, including the brutal reactionary chaos of jihadist Islam, which seems bent on ensuring patriarchy whatever the cost.

As Friedman outlines in *The World Is Flat: A Brief History of the Twenty-First Century*, America is the tent pole holding up this "big tent" of freedom, as China languishes in the hypocritical world of official communism powered by nepotistic capitalism and Russia seeks to be a Tsarist power, with nukes under the sway of crony capitalist robber barons that would put post-Reconstruction America to shame. It's herky-jerky and helter-skelter, but like a tumbleweed in a gale, the powers of equality are moving forward.

The challenge for America is to resolve its head-in-the-sand fear of change, as exemplified by the Tea Party and its barely legal collusion between politicos and Big Business, which is fueling the income disparities that are destroying the middle class. The silver lining to this dark cloud of American political obstructionism is that it is accelerating the alternate lifestyles of young people, and in the process rapidly dissolving gender roles in favor of a more equal sharing of home/work duties. These undercurrents of thought and belief are driving changes in our society, even as men and women themselves question how to go about it.

From one standpoint, the absence of true equality in society, in the workplace, and in attitudes may seem to indicate that progress toward gender equality is slow, but consider this: Women didn't even have the right to vote until 1920—even longer for women of color; they were effectively barred by discriminatory laws until the Voting Rights Act of 1964. Florida and South Carolina didn't get around to ratifying the Nineteenth Amendment allowing women to vote until 1969, followed two years later by Georgia and Louisiana, in 1971. Mississippi didn't ratify it until 1984!

For centuries, Anglo-Saxon common law held that a man could beat his wife as long as he did her no permanent physical harm, giving rise to the saying "rule of thumb," that a man could beat his wife with a stick no larger than the diameter of his thumb. While there is no specific reference to that phrase in English law, except in American courts, in *Commentaries on the Laws of England* (1765), Blackstone states that a man is allowed to "wound his wife severely with whips and fists" or other "corrective punishment." While wife beating was outlawed in the United States and England in the 19th century, it wasn't until the 1970s that feminists prevailed upon courts to discontinue treating spousal abuse as a private issue, separate from other cases of assault.[18]

Today, any modern couple would be horrified at condoning spousal abuse. However, it remains the leading cause of injury for women in the United States, and stories in the media of prominent male stars and sports figures beating their wives and girlfriends—and even being accused of killing them—are prolific.

Women's views of women's roles have changed rapidly, while men's views of male-female relations have lagged. The sociological literature shows that in a survey of high school seniors in 1976, only 42 percent of women disagreed with the statement: "It is usually better for everyone involved if the man is the achiever outside the home and the woman takes care of the home and family." In 1998, 71 percent of women disagreed with that statement.[19] However, showing how out of touch men are with the attitudes of their female counterparts, among male high school seniors, opposition to that statement grew from 17 percent to only 37 percent during that period.

Similarly, disagreement with the statement "The husband should make all the important decisions in the family" rose from 72 percent to 85 percent among women during that period, but remained virtually steady among men, with less than half disagreeing (a change from 44 percent to 49 percent).

One could say that a lot of men today are stuck in a 1950s view of women's roles. For a reminder of attitudes back then, the sociological literature also reveals a 1957 national survey that found that 80 percent of respondents considered a woman who remained unmarried to be "sick, neurotic, or immoral." In 1950, only 1 percent of Americans aged 20–29 lived alone. Today, 28 percent of all households consist of just one person, the highest level in US history.[20]

For men, it may seem like the old patterns are familiar, time tested, and supposed to be true. However, they just don't work anymore. What's wrong with women, anyway?

Why do women choose to live without men? A 1999 study of minority single mothers in urban settings found that women in a nonmarital relationship often felt that they had more control than if they had married. As David T. Ellwood and Christopher Jencks of the John F. Kennedy School of Government at Harvard University report, even if the couple cohabited, they nearly always lived with the woman's mother or in an apartment with the woman's name on the lease. Thus, mothers had the power to evict fathers if they interfered with childrearing, or if they tried to take control of the financial decision making, or if there was even a hint of spousal abuse. When asked what they liked best about being a single parent, their most frequent response was "I am in charge," or "I am in control."[21]

Given the disparity in attitudes about gender equality between men and women, it's no wonder many women are choosing to live apart from men. But as the imperative toward more freedom and equality continues to express itself, men will have to change, or find themselves increasingly isolated and talking to each other—beating their own drums and slapping each other on the back—while their effectiveness and status in society continues to erode. It is this disparity that prompts such books as *The End of Men*, with no small measure of truth attached.

Our social systems are reflecting the fact that Jesus's message of hope for men and women—all the little children of the world—is finally being heard. That the great political philosophers of the 17th and 18th centuries are finally being taken at their word. That freedom and equality really are inalienable rights for all people. And that the views of Adam Smith may unintentionally turn out to be the most effective feminist blueprint for our time.

These historical imperatives are just as strong, or stronger, than they were with the burgeoning democracies of two centuries ago, but they continue to play out in myriad ways that may seem baffling while they are occurring. Our job is to not get caught up in the archaic language, mores, and roadblocks of the past in negotiating contemporary conditions, but to adapt and thrive as new notions of equality, freedom, wealth, and faith emerge.

EXERCISE 1: *Heroes*

We love our heroes. We marvel at them, adore them, model ourselves after them and, often, after we have seen their feet of clay, we spurn them until the next hero appears. Who are your heroes?

They could include figures as diverse as Malcolm X and Ronald Reagan, Nelson Mandela, and Confederate general Robert E. Lee. Or film heroes, such as Harrison Ford of *Indiana Jones* fame, or Bluto in *Animal House*. Or music stars such as Bono or John Lennon.

List them, then note why this person is a hero. For example, with Bono you might not only admire his musicality but his charitable causes. What makes this person a hero to you? And how has this person changed your life?

EXERCISE 2: *The Hero's Journey*

In every man's life there is the hero's journey: the events, experiences, and tests that define him as the man he becomes.

What are tests that you endured that made you the man you are today? It might be easier to list the "firsts" of your life, such as first beer, first car, first deer (if you're a hunter), first date, and move on from there. Other significant events in your journey into manhood might be losing your virginity, landing your first job, your bar mitzvah, or getting patched (accepted) by a motorcycle club. Significant events might be having a fistfight in elementary school, going to war, or being robbed or assaulted. Not all of the major, transformative events in one's life are positive, nor do they end once a person reaches a certain age. Later in life, it can be seeing your child go off to school, giving your daughter away in marriage, losing a loved one through death or divorce. List them. What are the lessons you learned?

Would you say that the lessons you thought you learned then are the same lessons that you would draw today?

EXERCISE 3: *Explaining Role Models*

A common view in child rearing is that men don't want their sons to be "wusses" or sissies, while women want their sons to have some compassion, to not be cruel. Do you consider this to be fair? What if your son is gay or transgender or your daughter lesbian and intent on being treated without gender roles imposed? Would you be upset if your son or daughter were discriminated against for his/her gender? How would you explain to your son what it means to be a man?

EXERCISE 4: *Archetypes and Narratives of Sex and Aggression*

China's Communist Party tells the tale of the Fragrant Concubine in remote Kashgar, at the Afaq Khoja Mausoleum, where busloads of tourists come to pose with an actress dressed like a princess reminiscent of Walt Disney's famous characters. Among other sights, the *New York Times* reports, they come to see the tomb belonging to Iparhan, a Uighur imperial consort, who, according to legend, was so sweetly fragrant that she caught the attention of a Chinese emperor 2,700 miles away in Beijing.

"The love between her and the Qianlong emperor was so strong, after she died, he sent 120 men to escort her body back here for burial," one guide explained, eliciting smiles from the crowd. "It was a journey that took three years." But local residents offer a starkly different version, describing Iparhan as a tragic figure, little more than a sex slave who was dragged away from her home by soldiers and murdered by the emperor's mother after she repeatedly rejected Qianlong's advances, the *Times* reports.[22] Exalted princess or kidnapped sex slave? A tale of two narratives.

One is a love story, a fairy tale of a beautiful maiden promoted throughout the land to give a kinder, gentler face to an ugly legacy. The other is hidden, whispered, but known as true by those who live in the region; they say she isn't even buried there, as claimed.

We all live with narratives that explain our actions, our beliefs. Some are true, some not so true, and some are false. Some, such as the prince and princess archetype, mask ugly realities—but we prefer to cling to them, even basing our thoughts, beliefs, and actions on them.

This is a classic archetype of sexual conquest, seen from the dominator view as a romance and from an egalitarian view as sexual enslavement.

CONSIDER:
- Does this woman have a choice in her life circumstances?
- What role is she being forced to play?
- What are your views on stories about harems?
- Ask your wife, girlfriend, sister, mother, daughter, aunt, or other significant female friend or relation about her views on this story. How do they differ from your own?

What are the narratives in your life? How do they reflect your views on:
- Masculinity?
- Male-Female relations?
- Dating and romance?
- Ask your significant female friends and relations these questions. See how they differ from your own.

These questions are not asked to judge, but to allow an evolution in thought and belief toward more inclusive and richer understandings of intimacy and behavior.

Exercises: for Couples to Heal
Sexual Trauma and Build Intimacy

Christiane Northrup, M.D., in her book *Women's Bodies, Women's Wisdom*, gives a powerful exercise for men and women to help heal sexual trauma through intimate massage. She explains that the exercise, developed by Charles Muir and Caroline Muir, involves very gentle touch, while the partner gives 100 percent of his or her attention to the comfort of the receiving partner. Gentle massaging in a loving atmosphere connects one's genitals with one's heart. It also can be a catharsis, as old pains, guilts, and traumas are released energetically. Couples should proceed slowly and allow tears to be shed, with much holding of each other, as laughter and delight emerge.

Couples may also facilitate their own healing and development by helping each other obtain balance in their sexual perceptions. Sharing intimacy through mutual exploration can bring couples together and help them understand themselves better, as well.

For example, a few simple activities are included here:

SHARE A SHOWER: Rubbing each other with soap and the cleansing action of water can be a joyful experience. Set the intention to wash away old energies, attachments, and unwanted energetic debris left over from the workspace, previous activities, or even previous lifetimes.

SHARE ENERGY: After you have taken a shower together, go to a quiet spot where you will not be interrupted or distracted. If in an urban area, you may consider putting on a CD or iTune of "white noise" to block outside noise such as traffic, sirens, and the like. Set aside 10 minutes, no more. If you are totally present, you will find that intimate contact can stretch time, allowing a depth you have perhaps not noticed before. Time will mean nothing.

Remain naked and sit facing each other with the other's feet in your lap. Open your awareness so that you truly are seeing the whole person who is there before you. Look into each other's eyes, and allow yourself to let down your defenses. Be open. Look for the beauty in the other person, the "true face." Allow this openness to strengthen the connection between you, the bond that you share as human beings. Do not force energy at the other person, or project energy. Simply remain open, allowing your feelings to come forward.

You may find it difficult to "open up." You may find that your face wants to keep a guarded countenance, or your partner may find this and maintain a mask that does not reveal the true face. Don't force it if openness doesn't happen after a few minutes. If that happens, call a timeout. Discuss your feelings. What is coming up? What is preventing openness. Don't allow blame to shut either of you down. Seek understanding, so that you can repeat the exercise another time, with happiness and understanding.

The purpose of the exercise is to share who you are with another and feel the energy of the other in a good way. If there are barriers to openness, discuss what they are and how, or if, you wish to resolve them. If you do find openness, and sharing, without barriers, enjoy the moment. Repeat from time to time to keep your connection alive.

After you are through, clear yourself energetically by either using sage or a wand or simply brushing energetic debris off each other,

using Reiki or a feather. Set the intent: Thank you, Creator, for removing all footprints and debris from me and _____
(the name of the other) and returning it where it belongs. Thank you for transmuting all negativity into healing love and light.

MEDITATE ON THE YONI: If you have an intimate female partner, a wonderful source of discovery and growth can be found at your fingertips, so to speak.

In history, the yoni, or orifice of the female, has been venerated as the source of life. In depictions around the world, the vagina is seen as a great force for life giving and a symbol of the Creator. Only in the patriarchal view has the female sex organ been derided and degraded as in any way negative. The word "taboo" itself means "sacred," but the menstrual period deemed taboo by many cultures has been twisted to mean "unclean."

In fact, in traditional Native society, women in their "moon time," or menstrual period, were considered closer to the Creator than men, and imbued with special powers to divine secrets and foresee the future. This view of women as having great medicine and wisdom was prevalent throughout the world prior to the Romans. Men in today's culture have a number of slang terms that are hateful about the appearance, shape, and utility of the vagina, but it is a remarkable piece of natural art that also holds subliminal messages and ancient associations that are encoded in the DNA.

If your partner is willing, set aside a quiet time and space for intimacy, but of a different sort than may be routine. Perform the cleansing shower and then repair while naked to a private place, perhaps with quiet music, and have your partner lie on her back with her knees up and legs spread, draped from the waist down. This creates a "tent" of private space. Set aside 10 minutes, with your partner keeping the time.

Enter that tent, and simply observe the yoni. Do not touch. Simply place your attention on the vagina, and keep your mind clear of thoughts. The purpose of the tent is so that you will not be distracted by your partner's face or expressions. In this moment of quiet, once all the mental chatter has dissipated, you will find yourself drawn into a silent dialogue. The physical yoni will cease to be the object of your projections of sexuality or remembered notions of prejudice or preconceived ideas, and in the quiet, the shapes and reality of the sex organ will begin to draw out subtle and profound insights that may at first be wordless.

After the session, and in coming hours, days, and weeks, the lessons of simply observing and finding a meditation spot with this great symbol of life will continue to arise in your consciousness. Repeat the exercise as needed, and when both partners are amenable to it, and share the joy. Express your lessons to your partner, and switch, so that this time you are in the tent while she is observing your manhood.

The dialogue that can ensue can be quite revealing—not only about wrong perceptions, preconceived notions, and cultural upbringing but about new lessons and insights arising from the universal mind. All sacred spots offer the opportunity for people to enter all-time, no-time, or that space in prayer, visioning, and shamanic journey when the clock stops and time becomes a deep well of insight; you may be pleasantly surprised by the depth of knowledge obtained.

DRUM AS ONE: You will need a hand-held drum, such as a Remo 18-inch Buffalo drum or similar instrument, often used for shamanic journeying. Set aside 30 minutes for this exercise.

If you have an intimate female partner, a great way to get "in sync" is to drum together, as one heart beating. Perform the cleansing shower and then repair while naked to a private place, perhaps with quiet music, as in the previous exercises.

This time, though, first repeat the face-to-face exercise to remove masks and create openness, then once that 10-minute session is complete, have your partner sit in your lap facing outward. You will be sitting up and "spooning" with her back and shoulders at your chest, your face over her shoulder, and her buttocks on your lap, or on the floor if that is more comfortable, with your genitals touching her back.

In this posture, reach around her and pick up the drum. Rub the skin of the drum in a clockwise, circular motion to warm it, then begin gently drumming. Vary the cadence until you feel that your hearts are in sync. Move the drum slowly up and down and notice how the timbre, or pitch, of the drum varies as it passes over the chakra points.

If you were doing this alone, it would be considered an exercise of chakra balancing, but since you are together, it will help put you in sync with the earth's great heart energy, and with each other, as well as balance the chakras. Clear your mind of all chatter, and feel the wash of energy rise through and out your crown chakra; feel the energy in your body become harmonious and the rush of energy that radiates out from you as a couple through time and space.

After you begin to feel the effects waning, perhaps your arms become tired from holding the drum or drumming, gently bring the drumming to a stop. Share your thoughts feelings, impressions, and visions with your partner. Some couples find that this can create a type of energetic orgasm that radiates from both bodies and, once this ritual has been done, they can "connect" in thought, dream, and journey, even if separate by many miles, unless the energetic cords thus created are intentionally severed. [23]

From the Author's Notebook

Labels Hold Us Back

WE GET TOO HUNG UP ON LABELS. A few years ago, we had a quote on our website that summed it up from the BC cartoon by Hart: "A label is something you put on people so you can hate them without having to get to know them first."

I know for a fact that there are women who are physically stronger than I am, but I think I'm a fairly average male. I know that there are women who are much tougher than I am in confronting pain and enduring hardship, yet these are traits that are considered "manly." There are career pursuits that women are filling that traditionally have been the province of males, from police officer to firefighter to doctor, lawyer, and yes, Indian chief. To define manhood by career role or even mental disposition is a false model. There are men who are physically weak, mentally indecisive, even artistic—all once defined as primarily feminine traits. It does not make a man less of a man to be able to write poetry that evokes deep emotion or a woman less of a woman to be able to take a tough line as a prosecutor in a courtroom.

To even bring up these examples seems archaic and out of place in today's world, but they are ideas and archetypes floating around that affect thoughts, behaviors, and judgments. Dealing in such distinctions is difficult, and it puts the work of the definer of such traits in a paradox: If one tries to define characteristics usually attributed to men or women, then is not one participating in the very sexual stereotyping one is attempting to eliminate? One writer has suggested elevating such distinctions to virtues, to be subject to neutral choice. But it begs the question, how do you characterize the virtues or even possibility of, say, a feminist Hell's Angel? Is the biker's "bitch seat" now up front?

Perhaps we cannot control how some in society view one trait over another. I do know that characteristics of males and females are not separate; they are a continuum that overlaps—they are likely to be found at either extreme. So, in that case, we can control how we each view ourselves and each other, and we can let social norms follow the behavior of individuals rather than individuals trying to conform to pejorative and behavior altering labels. It should be a universal truth conveyed by all mothers and fathers to their offspring: Don't let others define you. Be who you are. That is the way of freedom.

Review

Seeing through the dysfunction in our society:

- Recognize, as Native American tribes determined centuries ago, warrior status should be limited, as should war.
- Acknowledge that if everyone actually lived according to the New Testament, the world would be a much more considerate, compassionate, and loving place.
- Recognize that even our mainstream spiritual understandings have been twisted to promote male archetypes that channel men into restrictive roles and relegate our mothers, wives, sisters, and daughters into subordinate roles.
- Recognize that the great tides of Christianity, democracy, and capitalism are inexorably moving the world toward a more equal society.
- Accept that men will have to change, or find themselves increasingly isolated and talking to each other, while their effectiveness and status in society continues to erode.
- Men and women can help each other heal and evolve through intimate massage and energy medicine techniques.

INTERNET KEY WORDS: *Essenes, Gnostics, The Nag Hammadi, Council of Nicea, archetypes, Occupy Wall Street, The End of Men, energy medicine*

New Archetypes
for a New World

Your old road is rapidly agin'…
Get out of the new one if you can't lend a hand
For the times they are a changin'.

— BOB DYLAN

As we have discussed, old archetypes don't apply. Rather than Iron John and Wild Man, our culture needs men who are compassionate, rational, intuitive, and judicious in their use of force. They do not traffic in fear and anger as the means to a self-serving end, promoting patriarchy and domination, but see the world as a place of competing choices where responsibilities are shared and impacts of behavior are carefully assessed.

As noted earlier, our Western society has been out of balance since Roman times, while Native American and other indigenous societies adhered more closely to a natural way of being. Those traits of responsibility toward the whole, providing for the people, and representing the ideas of the whole group, not an elite or select, powerful few, are traits badly needed in the modern world.

No longer does being male offer a free pass to be thoughtless, wanton, ignorant, or unflinching in projecting indiscriminate power. The modern male is no longer a king, unless one assumes he shares the crown. He is not a lover any more than his partner, with whom he shares intimacy. And he must not allow himself to be a warrior, in a constant state of war, which warps our sense of society and social obligations, unless he chooses to be and the social good demands it.

The modern male recognizes that peace, not war, is the natural state of humankind, that all human beings, regardless of roles or social stature, are stakeholders in the future of the planet, along with all the other beings of the earth, and that living in balance is the way of all nature.

Two examples of contrasts in manhood emerging in this new world are U.S. Presidents George W. Bush and Barack Obama.

George W. Bush clearly exemplified the very worst of the "old male"—bent on war, adamant in thought and behavior, reckless in the use of power, unmindful of the serious financial, human, and cultural costs and consequences of his actions. He showed his status as a man-child, uncomfortable in his own skin and trying to "out-macho" his peers, through adolescent posturing, incomprehensible thought processes expressed in linguistic blundering, an inability to carve his own path, except in rebellious rejection of his own father's diplomacy, and in his need to seek approval from another more forceful, warlike, unbending patriarchal figure in the form of his ostensible subordinate Vice President Dick Cheney.

George Bush is a poster child for a man gone wrong. We see it in his dissolute youth, his careless and irresponsible young adulthood, his posturing and bluster, his misuse of facts to support his claim to be a "war president" and conqueror, and his born-again piety, which served to advance his agenda of turning back women's rights and reinforcing power elites.

His legacy is one of repression, regression, and fear under the guise of wielding power and exercising control, whether it be authorizing torture, supporting domestic spying, destroying the balance of power in the Middle East, overextending the treasury, retarding human and gender rights, or engendering a veer to the right in religious, economic, and social measures in government. His base was the angry white male who is losing his grip in representative government, religion, and economic hegemony.

By contrast, President Obama came into power as the anti-Bush, promising peace, inclusiveness, a rejection of power elites in favor of civil rights, human rights, social rights, and the broadening of government service for minorities, the historically underserved, and the middle class.

Whereas George Bush epitomized a rejection of the historical imperatives of more democracy, more equality, and more inclusiveness in government, capitalism, and religion, Obama exemplified them: a minority male who was not "macho" in his behavior, who was thoughtful, mindful of others, careful in his actions, operating on a consensus model of governance, and with goals that weigh the benefits to the whole as more important than the few.

While some may criticize Obama as being too moderate in his words and behaviors, too tentative, too accommodating, and too willing to compromise, these behaviors are ones that tend to most successfully serve the marginalized, the historically voiceless, the co-alitions of under-represented in all their diversity. Obama's is a voice of reason and logic, of carefully planning and executing a path of inclusiveness. His base is diverse in terms of race, gender, ethnicity, more female than male, and more compassionate and inclusive—those who are on the ascendancy in the historical thrust toward more equality and sharing of power.

The focus of this book is not to create new archetypes; it is to help individuals define themselves, based on spiritual and common-sense principles that have guided humankind in societies around the globe for thousands of years. In this way, new archetypes can emerge naturally. This is not so much about the rise of a new male as a new incarnation of the male; one that harkens back to the way men have been before our world got so out of kilter—in harmony with women, elders, children, and other men and responsible stewards of their world.

As with the real-life examples of Presidents Bush and Obama, if this book helps develop new archetypes for a new world, what would those archetypes be? Or approximate? Which archetypes would be useful and which would be deleterious to the positive aims and needs of society?

A strong archetype in popular culture is the cowboy of the Old West. As portrayed in Westerns, this Lone Ranger has an unfortunate connection with guns and women as victims, as well as men who are loners without connection to society. It is an archetype that is also found in detective novels. The hero always has the highest of motives (protecting women, defeating evil), along the lines of a spiritual quest to bring justice to the world, but he usually does it by violent means.

Based on fear, these types of literature provide portraits of angry men in an angry world. Their relationships are a form of celibate exile while they pursue higher "manly" values, alleviated by brief relationships with bigger-than-life (unattainable, perfect, goddess-like or terribly flawed, helpless without their intervention) females. These are not flesh-and-blood, living, breathing, mother/sister/daughter human beings. These are basically airbrushed pinups with a gun as a masturbatory tool.

Nonetheless, the reluctantly celibate, savior monk archetype of the loner may be a new reality for many men today, not by choice but as a result of new mores. For many young people today, relationships aren't formed in dates so much as groups hanging out together and "hooking up"—one-night stands without emotional commitment. Marriage is often put off until a woman's fertile years are almost over, so that she can establish her career and income. The rise of single mothers suggests that parenthood may be a goal among such women, but without marriage or traditional family.

As a result, more Americans are living alone than ever before, and men are pretty much left to their own devices. Archetypes for men living alone are powerful but few, and outdated. They too fully support the "absent male" dynamic explored earlier with "the father wound" and "dark mother."

With men and women living increasingly apart, what defines masculinity is a subject of concern among male adolescents. This has particularly negative implications for intimacy and contraception, and should raise flags with both men and women about the future of healthy heterosexual relationships.

The absence of parental males from family units is becoming well documented. It is blamed for problems among young people, including drug abuse, low self-esteem, poor grades in school, and violence. The children in such families are more likely to be poor, exhibit anxiety and depression, and drop out of school. The offspring of absent fathers often turn to forming substitute families through gang involvement and teen pregnancy, which foster aberrant views of women as objects, not as living, breathing human beings who share space and humanity with men.

Seeing women as objects translates to more sexual partners, a less intimate relationship with the current sexual partner, and through the absence of respect toward women, greater belief that relationships between women and men are adversarial. These behaviors are linked to low condom use, less belief in male responsibility to prevent pregnancy, and greater belief that pregnancy validates masculinity, even to the detriment of the sexual partner. [1]

Males without father figures practice casual sex more often because it fits with a "macho" image; they do not respect females and do not view sex as either special or meaningful. They use women and sexual relationships as a means of achieving pleasure and gaining popularity with their peers.[2]

The adverse effects are not limited to male children; female children develop differently without a father, as well. Promiscuity, out-of-wedlock births, and anxiety over social relationships are frequent outcomes of the lack of a positive male figure in the home. Among other positive influences, a father shapes his daughter's views of male and female bonds and sexual relationships, instills self-respect, and demonstrates that she deserves other men's love and respect without having to rely on sexual attraction alone.[3]

But even in stable relationships, the loner male or rebel figure is tragically maladapted to a caring, sharing, responsible role. Many young women know all too well about "making do" or "settling" for an underachieving, uneducated male with a sense of privilege heightened by low self-esteem. While regional archetypes may vary, in the South, the rebel outlaw may be known as a "good ole boy" more interested in smoking dope, drinking whiskey, and shooting guns than being available to share household duties. If he is more laid back, he may be more interested in lying on the couch, smoking cigarettes, and drinking beer than finding, or keeping, gainful employment.

Often self-defined "losers," such men find plenty of reasons for underachieving, with varied excuses to avoid work or responsibility. In maturity, these good ole boys are lazy, greedy, and opportunistic, usually quite proud of their ability to "go along to get along," and keep the "old boy network" in good working order. They form the bulk of the rearguard action against "radical ideas" to promote equality, in maintaining attitudes and social institutions enforcing male (and often racial) discrimination.

In small towns and rural areas across the South, in former years, they could be seen sitting in idled cars and pickup trucks waiting for their wives to get off their shifts at textile mills, especially on payday, when a stop before home would be the liquor store to stock up. Generations of Southern politicians, from Theo G. Bilbo in Mississippi, to George Wallace in Alabama, to Lester Maddux in Georgia, to such national figures as Ronald Reagan (with his "welfare queen" analogies) have catered to this world of underachieving, low-education, low-income white males.

When the loser life reaches its lowest point, prison is the result— usually a consequence of more bad choices, which may include murder of the spouse (often after years of domestic abuse during which law enforcement authorities looked the other way). This is the stuff of which country music is made.

And even if the man works, the refrain of losing and loss and drowning one's sorrows may still be countered by a reactionary roller-coaster religious zeal. This dictates that one can be a sinner all week, cheating and drinking and doing wrong, as long as there's forgiveness on Sunday: a dance of sin and forgiveness that repeats itself again and again, as long as religion is rote and spirituality is absent. There is no end of opportunities for doing wrong or second chances under the watchful eye of the sinners in the hands of an angry (male) god archetype.

The unexamined life may not be worth living, but it's alive and well in the South—with regional variants, in both rural and urban areas across America.

Even in high-achieving households, the absent father, as exemplified by the "father wound," produces flawed examples of male development. Both men and women are victims of the real-life archetypes common in this country today, as women take on more responsibilities for absent males while at the same time expecting little from their partners, and men fail to reach their full potential, eschewing responsibility. It's a cycle that produces dysfunctional relationships across generations.

An Alternate Model from Native America

Sometime between AD 1000 and AD 1500, before King John signed the Magna Carta in England and long before the first European set foot on the shores of the North American continent, a society evolved in the northeastern section of North America that would become one of the most peaceful, ordered civilizations on the face of the earth. Early European colonists marveled at its system of democratic laws, at its unheard-of equality, at its pastoral peace, and at its unity and strength as a confederation of peoples. The settlers called these Native people the Iroquois; they called themselves the Haudenosaunee, or The People of the Longhouse.

Their government was called the Iroquois Confederacy, comprising initially the northeastern tribes that made up the Five Nations of the Iroquois (later Six Nations): the Mohawk, Onondaga, Oneida, Cayuga, Seneca, and Tuscarora. The Iroquois Confederacy influenced the thoughts and writings of Benjamin Franklin, Thomas Jefferson, and James Madison. It served as the example for Revolutionary America's Albany Plan, the Articles of Confederation and, ultimately, the U.S. Constitution.

Today, this influence, if mentioned at all, is only considered a footnote in American history, its originator all but forgotten. But this pre-Columbian Native American society deserves remembering because it offers what today could be the essentials of a perfect society, embodying social equality, military strength, effective diplomacy, and spiritual power. It might sound Utopian, and in some ways, it purposely set out to be that way. It remains a model from which we can learn much. Indeed, with the changes under way in society regarding gender roles, we may already be headed toward a less perfect, unintentional version of this society. With a conscious push toward its higher ideals, we might improve our society and build on the concepts embodied by this ancient way of life.

The Iroquois Confederacy was a true democracy, based on health, happiness, and spirituality, and it had a constitution from which all of its authority emanated. Like most Native American societies, it was matrilineal, meaning its customs, laws, and kinship were based on the mother's family. It honored the Earthly Mother and Spiritual Father, which may have made it difficult for Christian Europeans, so deeply entrenched in their patriarchal god and culture, to accept. But, if the Iroquois system of laws—legal and spiritual—had been embraced by the early colonists, we would probably have a far more representative, peaceful, and powerful country than we have today.

The Messenger, Deganawidah, was the founder of their system of laws and religion. He was known as the Man from the North, or, simply, the Peacemaker. From what has been handed down through the generations, his life has eerie parallels with that of Jesus.

Like Jesus's grandmother, Anne, Deganawidah's maternal grandmother also had an angel of the Great Spirit visit her in a dream and tell her that her daughter would give birth to a messenger of God. Both mother and daughter were told that the coming child would be an incarnation of the Great Spirit sent to do His work.

The story of Deganawidah's acts is as filled with meaning as the recorded miracles of Christ, each event proving to the Native American peoples that he was blessed. His message was clear when he told them: "I speak for the Master of Life, and the word that I bring is that all people shall love one another and live together in peace."

Deganawidah appeared in a time of social chaos, filled with war. To bring his message to the people, Deganawidah enlisted the support of a respected woman of good heart named Jigonhsasee, who lived at a well-traveled crossroads between the various tribes.

She always opened her lodge to whoever needed a place to rest and fed them. In her house, even the men of tribes that were bitter enemies laid down their weapons and made peace as long as they were under her roof.

She would come to be known as the Mother of Nations.

It was Jigonhsasee who advised Deganawidah on how to get along with the tribes and, in order to do that, she advised that he find someone who could speak eloquently on his behalf.

Deganawidah, you see, was not a perfect man. He was a stutterer. Although he was forced to choose his words carefully, each carrying deep meaning, they were marred by his impediment.

The message: We all must reach out to fulfill our truth.

The man who came to be Deganawidah's spokesman was a hermit and cannibal, feared by all of the Iroquois. After Deganawidah taught this fearsome human creature to see his own True Face (his authentic self) through compassion and forgiveness, the cannibal became a new man, with a new name: the great orator Hayenwatha.

Hayenwatha become the voice of Deganawidah.

Together, they embarked on their mission of peace, converting even the most feared evil sorcerer of all: Tadodaho.

Tadodaho was feared by all of the Five Nations of the Iroquois Confederacy. He was able to cast magic spells with his words, snare the unwary, terrify the mighty, and confound even the greatest intellects.

Tadodaho was grotesquely deformed, with a misshapen body. He hated himself, and he hated others, believing that everyone was out to "get" him. This was probably true, for Tadodaho had living snakes for hair and invaded peoples nightly dreams with murder, torture, and cannibalism, driving the people mad.

With the help of their followers in the various tribes they had converted, with their unity and strength behind them, Deganawidah through Hayenwatha answered the prayers of the people by convincing Tadodaho of the error of his ways. In return, Tadodaho was made the most powerful of all the tribal elders, revered as responsible for them acting correctly.

The governmental position of Tadodaho was enshrined in Iroquois law. And each of the tribes held seats on the council designated by the name of the one who first held that seat, so their stories would not be forgotten and their lessons would be honored in every decision.

In this way, the Peacemaker teaches that our greatest fears and barriers can become our strongest allies; that war, confusion, and strife can be conquered by extending peace, understanding, and inclusion; and that even diametrically opposed elements that threaten chaos and ruin can be blended to make a stronger, more unified whole.

It is noteworthy that the converted cannibal Hayenwatha (also known as Hiawatha in English retellings), who became the soothing, eloquent spokesman of peace, was the one who combed the snakes from Tadodaho's hair to make him the administrator of peace rather than the instigator of nightmares. Through wise words, reason, honor, and understanding, his body became uncontorted and he assumed a new stature, both physically and in the esteem of all the people. Through this form of forgiveness, compassion, and prayer, he was healed in body, mind, and spirit.

There are valuable lessons here for making a true democracy: inclusion; recognizing and honoring diversity; seeing people's strengths and not their weaknesses; and convincing everyone that a system of justice, balance, and integrity can calm any situation or allow the best course of action to be chosen. Most importantly, there is strength in the unity of hearts and minds.

The Peacemaker devised a system of checks and balances to ensure that the newly united tribes, whose territories spanned hundreds of miles in the Northeast, from Canada to the Chesapeake

Bay, would always live in peace. These comprised three primary principles: righteousness, health, and power.

RIGHTEOUSNESS meant that individuals and nations should always act in accordance with justice. This formed not only the impetus for belief but also included the expectation that actions should be judged by the custom of right action.

HEALTH meant that there should be a balance between body and mind, developing an inner peace that comes from nurturing minds that are free and at ease.

POWER includes authority and autonomy. That would seem a contradiction, but it's based on spiritual power, *orenda*, a power that is greater than any individual or any society.

This creative force of life, or true spiritual power, is a dualism made up of individual freedom bound by responsibility to self and others. As with male and female qualities, when tapped by an individual or community this dualism produces an outcome greater than the sum of its parts. For its power lies in the concept of justice, as opposed to enshrined law. It is living and changing, not static or able to be outlived. This power comes from within, not imposed from without.

Deganawidah gave the people the eagle as their symbol, for it was far-seeing and could discern trouble from a distance. It soars among the heavens and is guided by the Great Spirit. It has wisdom and strength.

Deganawidah gave the people the Tree of Peace as the symbol of the confederacy, the Living Agreement that must be nurtured, and which, if tended, would shelter them and provide roots for the generations of their people yet to come.

After the people adopted his way of peace, Deganawidah said his work was done. He simply disappeared. But, thereafter, it was known that whenever one wanted to speak to the Peacemaker, all one had to do was to speak into the wind or the trees and he would hear them and offer guidance.

The parallels between the life of the Peacemaker and the life of Jesus and the teachings they both gave are phenomenal.

Deganawidah taught what he called "Good News, A New Mind, A High Peace." He taught love, forgiveness, compassion, and prayer in a time of great turmoil. He took the highest spiritual principles of the people and applied them to their daily life. He created a society that could live in harmony.

And what of the Iroquois symbols, the great Tree of Peace and the eagle?

The Nag Hammadi quotes Jesus in The Secret Book of John: "I appeared in the form of an eagle upon the Tree of Knowledge . . . I did this to teach the human beings, and to awaken them from deep sleep."

Foremost, Deganawidah taught that government can be spiritual and it can be just. It springs from the hearts and minds of the people.

Just as science is deemed entirely separate from spirituality in the modern world, government has lost its spiritual underpinnings, as well. As a result, various denominations have tried to capture government, with government, in return, resisting any attempt at spiritual influence.

The key message of the Iroquois Confederacy, as taught by Deganawidah, seems to have been lost: If the people adopt a spiritual life, the government will reflect the spiritual orientation of the people. Spirituality cannot be imposed by a government, but a government can reflect the spiritual principles of the people.

Deganawidah was not the god of the Iroquois; he was the Creator's messenger. And, like Jesus, Deganawidah is a great "reference being" for all peoples. Just as the early Christian Gnostics believed in Sophia, the Iroquois believed that the Female Deity in union with the Male Principle created Earth, and they gave her the name Sky Woman.

In both the Gnostic and Iroquois visions of the Creation, the Female Principle gives life, while the Male Principle gives direction and purpose. Each has its way of being, and neither could exist without the other. They are different but equal. Each has unique qualities. Neither is better than the other. Each is essential. Together, they create balance.

Deganawidah taught the tribes of the confederacy how to apply the female principle to their daily life. Like the Essenes of Jesus's time, theirs was an agrarian society with a belief that the source of all life was light, embodied by the sun. The Iroquois called the Heavenly Father "The Maker of Breath," for they believed the Life Force of God was in the breath (which in Oriental medicine is called *Ki*, or *Qi*). This power, the Life Force, connected all living things and connected each human with all living things.

Since the Creator embodied the Female Principle it was only right that life on Earth be ordered by the female in Deganawidah's view. He built a society founded on the Female Principle.

In the Sky World, the tree that Sky Chief tore from the ground to create Earth had four white roots stretching to each of the four directions: north, south, east, and west. From that beautiful tree, all good things grew.

The sons that the daughter of Sky Woman birthed were The Good Mind and The Evil Mind. And even today, all human beings must walk the path between the polarity of good and evil. A polarity, as the Essenes saw, exists only for humankind, not in the mind of God.

Since women were the fertile providers of life on Earth, Deganawidah entrusted them with the farming, house, and home: the fertility and bearing of the earth. And he incorporated the emotional richness of feminine life and family into the sometimes harsh decision-making of government in order to achieve balance.

In Iroquois society all property belonged to the women. Families lived in longhouses, which could be 100 feet long, in which each pair of parents had their own room and a large common area. Supreme in every family was the eldest woman, the "mother" of the household. She owned the longhouse in which all resided. When she died, the next eldest woman took over. All males left home as soon as they were married and lived in the longhouses of their wives. Except for a man's weapons, clothes, and personal possessions, all property belonged to the women, specifically, the eldest woman of each longhouse.

Thus the role of Elder Mothers was established in society and grounded by very real considerations. Her word was law within her household, as the household and everything in it and everything associated with it literally belonged to her.

Young men were reared by the women to be the leaders of the society, subject to review by the Elder Mothers. Those who held seats on the governing body were chosen through the Elder Mothers of the clans to represent their tribe. These representatives ruled at the discretion of the Elder Mothers, who nominated them, briefed them before each session, monitored their legislative record and, if necessary, removed them from office.

This offered a system of checks and balances in ruling the tribe, ensuring that every voice was heard and decisions were truly representative of the whole tribe, male and female, and for the benefit of the tribe, including children and future generations.

In fact, a ceremony during the deliberations included having a fan waved next to the council fire so that if arguments became heated, it would blow away "debris" that the future children of the tribe might trip over.

In modern terms, the Elder Women would be considered the legislature, for they were the property owners of the tribe. They decided matters of war and peace because, as the mothers of the warriors, they keenly knew what the tribe risked.

The warriors and other male societies would be considered the executive branch. They were free to do as they pleased, go on long hunting parties, war raids, or other activities, as long as it was condoned by the Elder Women of the tribe.

The judicial function was performed by *sachems*, chiefs who usually were men but could be women, selected by the Elder Women for their balance, temperament, and sense of justice. Since the Elder Women knew everyone in the tribe, their relations and their deeds throughout their lives, there was no question of not knowing who among the tribe was best suited for this function.

Today, the actual councils would be considered rather longwinded affairs. The Iroquois were extremely eloquent in their language, and considered every word uttered as true and thus worth considering. Each speaker was impeccable with his words. Words held power. No word was discounted. Every word was uttered with profound meaning.

To prove the truth of the speaker, when one in the council rose to speak, he held his *wampum*, or belt, which had embroidered on it all the great deeds of his clan. As long as he held the wampum, his words were considered truth, his greatest truth, and represented the word of his clan and tribe.

Thus, he was compelled to speak carefully and weigh every word, as it reflected not only upon himself but every relative, his ancestors, and future generations. He could assume the truth he told, if adopted by the people, would set the future, guiding his people to action.

That representative was allowed to speak until he felt no further words were necessary, then allowed to sit and reflect to ensure he left nothing out. Then, arising again, and holding the wampum to signify truth, he spoke until he felt all angles of the discussion from his tribe's viewpoint were expressed. There were no interruptions. In fact, early colonists were astounded by the courtesy extended each speaker.

Between orations, the tribes would caucus to discuss what they heard and what their "take" on the matter would be. Speeches would go on for hours, days, even weeks, until every viewpoint was expressed and consensus was found among the various viewpoints.

The Iroquois were, thus, a very compassionate, thoughtful, deliberative people in their official acts. Their councils were designed to seek peace at all costs and to honor the Tree of Peace, which was at the council site, the symbol Deganawidah had given them as their overriding goal of life.

But, when moved to war, they were the most fierce of any Native Americans in the region, for if the Iroquois decided to go to war, they would not stop until they won or literally died trying. If it were the will of the people to fight in order to ensure peace, they would not falter.

In family life, children were especially valued. Under Iroquois law, every child had an absolute right to adequate food, clothing, and shelter. Furthermore, each child was viewed as a blessing from the Creator and entitled to be treated with respect, dignity, and love.

Every girl child was groomed to become an Elder Woman. The boys were raised for independence, resiliency, and strength. Elder men who were too old to hunt acted as tutors and mentors for these young men. They would devise tests for the boys as way of determining what might be the young man's power animal or totem, a protector that could guide him spiritually in his daily doings.

At an early age, around 12 or 13 years, when the boy was entering adolescence, the elder man would take the young man into the woods for a vision quest. There, the young man would fast for days and attend to every aspect of what occurred around him. Visions the boy received during this time would instruct him on the nature of his being, his purpose in life, the tests he might face in the future, and what his value might be to the earth and to his society. That was his "coming of age."

In common with other Native American societies, the Iroquois recognized homosexuality as a relatively rare but natural fact in their society. They believed that those who had homosexual tendencies were neither male nor female, but a third gender. Rather than being ostracized, such individuals were carefully observed from childhood in order to determine their unique role in the Creator's plan.

This view, contrary to patriarchal and conservative religions, is also common in ancient societies around the globe. In the *Kama Sutra*, dating to the first century BC in India, with its origins possibly in the eight century BC, third-gender sexual relations are treated matter-of-factly and in great detail, with possible scenarios of sexual play and the roles often encountered in the Hindu society of the day. References to sexual conduct—both heterosexual and homosexual— as being pleasurable, even recreational, disappeared following invasions by Aryan marauders and succeeding Moslem influences, as did references to sexuality on *stele*, the large stone slabs used to record events in in India and other ancient civilizations. The texts are indicative of a view held also in Old Europe prior to Roman conquest that eroticism was a divine state, including all its diversity.

Most "third gender" Iroquois children were male so, as with the other young men of the tribes, the dreams of such young boys were carefully analyzed to determine their role in life. Often, third-gender boys were groomed as spiritual leaders of the community and acted as counselors and guides because they were believed to be especially touched by the Creator and closer to the Earthly Mother and Heavenly Father than most humans. They were not in any way forbidden to pursue their own sexuality, a fact that caused a great deal of consternation among European Christian missionaries.

This relaxed attitude toward gender roles was also found among early Christian Gnostics. In fact, one of the strains of Gnosticism (as detailed in the Nag Hammadi ancient texts) incorporated an androgynous male figure in the godhead.

In Iroquois society, all life was sacred—male, female, "third gender," animals, and plants. All were considered to be offspring of Grandmother Sky Woman's child, and as members of the family of Earth were worthy of respect. Among Native American societies, this life as we know it was only one reality—a reality that we share with all living beings here on Earth—but not the only reality. That reverence for life and human "being" in this one plane of existence is consistent with Gnostic, Essene, Hindu, Buddhist, and virtually all forms of human religious expression.

The hunting and killing of game for food by males of the tribe was an important part of Native American society, yet the men did not kill wantonly. They knew that every animal is possessed of the same divine spirit that lived within them. They personally thanked the animal for making the sacrifice so that the people might live, making offerings of cornmeal or tobacco to the earth to balance the exchange.

Young children often played together, even amorously. Early colonists were shocked by the open displays of affection. The young people felt in no hurry to get married, and they were advised to explore their own sexuality and partners before making a marriage decision.

It must be remembered that in Iroquois society, women were not property and did not require permission from a father to marry.

Women were, in fact, the property owners, and it was they who freely chose whether to marry. When a marriage was proposed, it was discussed by the Elder Women of each young person's clan. Then a simple ceremony was performed, and the young man moved in with the young woman in her clan's longhouse and became a member of that clan.

Divorce was simple, too. If a woman decided she no longer wanted the man, she set his belongings on the doorstep. The marriage was over. Since women owned everything, there was no question of division of property, alimony, or child support.

In Iroquois society, the "social security" of the elderly was provided gratefully. Elders—male and female—were respected for their wisdom and their contributions to the tribe. Their physical needs were cared for. The entire basis of the society was its concern for the whole tribe, the whole people, the group; if anyone suffered, the group suffered.

As a result of this rather "liberated" view of women's roles and power (especially in 17th- and 18th-century America), it was not uncommon for European women to flee to live with the tribes. Many of the stories we see on television and in movies about settler women being "kidnapped" actually involve women who in reality found this way of life more empowering and their lives far better than in the towns and cities of settlers.

The indigenous people of the Americas lacked technology; they didn't lack humanity. In many ways, they were more spiritual, more loving, more trusting, more open, certainly healthier, and more creative in their personal lives, their societies, and governments than the invaders.

In addition to the clans, the nations of the Iroquois Confederacy were also divided into *moieties,* or subgroups that represent the two sides of a particular equation affecting the life of the tribe. Among the Iroquois moieties were typically organized as "sides" to keep their society balanced through proscriptions on marriage; however, across North America, tribal moieties were, and still are, defined in different ways, such as by lineage, by a peer group, by season, or by the ways in which people work, worship, socialize, and observe states of war or peace. The themes used to characterize moieties provide social cohesion and help establish an individual's self-identity. Members may be recruited and confirmed by elaborate initiation ceremonies.

Modern Moieties Emerging By Choice

In a sort of "back to the future," the moiety approach might be the direction contemporary culture is headed, as women become single mothers, breadwinners, heads of household, and men become more intermittent in their lives. This holds much significance, even if it is unintentional.

If women increasingly live alone, with support groups of other women who are the property owners and wealth managers, and if they continue to ally themselves with men who hold less financial status, attainment, earning capacity, and educational development, then social relationships are certain to evolve. As a result, expect fewer marriages (or lasting marriages) and more social relationships that appear consistent with alliances found in Native American moieties, whether by blood or by choice, than traditional two-person matrimony.

In the same way, some social scientists believe modern society is moving toward a "new tribalism." This neotribalism will not be expressed in the pejorative sense of "us against them," or in lines of distinction or separation of one group from another, but in the form of open, egalitarian, classless, and cooperative intentional communities, whether they come together in a formalized way or on an ad hoc basis through friendship circles. This type of arrangement, they posit, is the natural state of humanity, going back thousands of years.

In this evolving friendship moiety, or "chosen family," men and women individually come together for love, companionship, and intimacy, or for economic security, but not necessarily with the aim of matrimony or the death-do-us-part approach found in the conventional model of marriage. Both partners may drift in and out of relationships, with perhaps multiple long-term relationships, which may or may not include children and a trip to the altar. In this emerging scenario, women remain the stable influence for children's development, as men drift in and out of the children's lives.

Whether these types of relationships exist within the formal structure of an intentional community, with a set space, elected leaders, rules, and so forth, or within loose, unstructured, friendship circles that may or may not last for decades, one thing is clear: the thrust of modern life seems to be toward less formal marriage and kinship arrangements, often based more on individual choices than family dictates or geography. The economies allowed by such arrangements include live-in arrangements for basic financial security within a set geographic area to collections of individuals with common interests, such as young professionals who move to new locales for economic reasons and come together as a collective for mutual support.

Nor is the concept of intentional communities limited by region. International groups have coalesced to lend support, provide information, and share strategies. For example, the Global Ecovillage Network (GEN) is a growing network of sustainable communities and initiatives that bridge different cultures, countries, and continents. GEN serves as an umbrella organization for ecovillages, transition town initiatives, intentional communities, and ecologically minded individuals worldwide. Website: *http://gen.ecovillage.org*.

The Fellowship For Intentional Community includes ecovillages, cohousing communities, residential land trusts, communes, student co-ops, urban housing cooperatives, intentional living, alternative communities, cooperative living, and other projects where people strive together with a common vision. Website: www.ic.org.

Young men need older men as well as peers in order to develop fully as mature men. They need to learn from older men, as well as feel a sense of belonging and respect from that group, in order to refine and perhaps redefine themselves as fully adult males with mature characteristics. Too many men today exhibit adolescent behaviors that, once they take hold, are difficult to change without constant interaction with adult males with mature sensibilities.

In the last century, this interaction was provided by social clubs where men could find a sense of belonging among older men with whom they shared work and family responsibilities. In the more rural South, some of the avenues of social maturation for young men were found in men-only hunting or fishing camps and clubs, where they would spend days together in the shared activity of hunting or fishing or caring for the camp. While it's true that excess alcohol consumption was often a companion activity, and many of the goings-on were (and are) rather bawdy, they provided a shared space of men of all ages to share their experiences and outlooks.

Unfortunately, the social networks that existed in the previous century for men's social clubs have mostly disintegrated, along with the sense of belonging to cultural groups that young men enjoyed, with negative effects on society.[4]

Today's upbringing is often by television, smartphone, or tablet or, in inner-city neighborhoods, if not by gangs then at the barbershop, one of the few truly socially integrating shared spaces for men.

For an entire generation, young people have been socialized into a never-ending war, with the military or outgrowths of homeland security police philosophies and supporting political thought forming the social attitudes of young men. These top-down, hierarchical, dominator ways of thinking do not allow room for diversity of thought or behavior, creative nonviolent solutions to problems, patience, or tolerance toward the inevitable ambiguities of life. Rather, since they stem from narrow rules and interpretations that require rigorous allegiance backed by social control, they are designed to reinforce certain behaviors, thoughts, beliefs, and approaches over others that can only be defined as adolescent.

This type of thinking inevitably leads to behaviors such as snap judgments based on training, rather than independent thought, belief, or experience. It leads to risky behaviors and simple, rote solutions to complex, perhaps insoluble problems or issues. It promotes the desire for instant gratification without regard to the thoughts, feelings, or outcomes for others. It feeds a constant need for positive reinforcement as part of the group, rather than independent thought and behavior. And it fosters the denial of facts when they don't fit preconceived notions.

Some observers have pointed out that young males' preoccupation with violent video games reinforces aggressive, short-sighted, two-dimensional views of life that are out of sync with more nuanced real-world experiences. The same could be said about young males' preoccupation with certain books, movies, or pornography in the extreme. For young men, life must be leavened by real-life experiences and honest, life-altering interactions with men.

In Native societies, such experiences were offered during the hunt, during war, and under the tutelage of spiritual leaders who would conduct sweat lodges, purification ceremonies, spirit clan initiations, and other activities, as well as the day-to-day instruction provided by the uncle to the young man and by his father. In today's emerging era of living in a moiety by choice, women may choose men in their lives who can help their offspring grow into manhood, and men should offer themselves to their significant loved ones to help their partner in the child's development. This could be the most important new archetype for this age: the "uncle" by choice.

Any man living today can look back and list the men in his life who taught him certain aspects of what it means to be a man in the realms of work, sex, marriage, and life in general. It's an important part of living and maturing. What's missing, however, is an update to those skills and lessons.

A Man's Home is His (Shared) Castle

Parenting is a vital role for men, as well as women. Archetypes must change because men's roles are changing. Men who have been laid off from factory jobs or as a result of outsourcing are choosing to stay at home and raise their children, while their wives, who may be more educated or trained in specialized, higher-paying jobs such as nursing, continue to work. One such laid-off factory worker explained his reasoning to *The New York Times*, "By the time I get a paycheck, it all goes to day care, or I can stay home and raise my own children."

While most stay-at-home parents are mothers, fathers represent a growing share of all at-home parents: 16 percent in 2012, up from 10 percent in 1989, according to according to a Pew Research Center analysis of U.S. Census Bureau data.[5]

Roughly a quarter of these stay-at-home fathers (23 percent) report that they are home mainly because they cannot find a job. Nearly as many (21 percent) say the main reason they are home is to care for their home or family. This represents a fourfold increase from 1989, when only 5 percent of stay-at-home fathers said they were home primarily to care for family. The figures take into account an economy rebounding from the Great Recession, and the analysis points to a long-term growth trend continuing toward more stay-at-home dads.

Pew also notes that while physical disability is a factor in stay-at-home dads, another issue that throws the figures into greater perspective as far as family makeup is concerned is the fact that a rising share of fathers do not live with their children at all. About 16 percent of fathers with young children lived apart from all of their children. These figures support the changing face of men's roles and that of the family itself.

One of the pitfalls that feminism has encountered, which the restructuring of men's roles and attitudes must seek to avoid, is the charge of classism. In her book *Lean In*, Facebook CEO Sheryl Sandberg raised the issue of changing roles in the highest levels of capitalism; however, critics have charged that Sandberg's message is pitched to professional elites rather than to the masses. Despite all the gains of women in society, including education, salary, and changing roles, the reality remains that women make up a growing proportion of the long-term unemployed and low-income women lead a growing majority of households headed by single mothers.

Rather than saying that feminism is a way to address these issues, it should be apparent that changing social mores should address them—not as women's issues but as serious issues facing society as a whole. And rather than looking at these issues as being about liberating all women, we should approach them as liberating men and women from archetypes that no longer serve the greatest good of society. In this instance, Sandberg's thesis is a sound one: self-improvement leads to individual empowerment—and that's true regardless of gender or class.

Today's economic and social pressures require two seemingly contradictory stances: individual empowerment and couples working together to overcome the barriers and challenges put before them. People flourish in relationship. The Lone Ranger does not exist. Today's economic realities are forcing couples to make changes they might not have considered only a decade ago.

For example, in *Lean In*, Sandberg notes that women today seem to be running a marathon, with bystanders often seeming to be telling them to quit. Consider two people, a man and a woman, who start the race together, but all along the way, the crowd is yelling for the man to win the race, while they are telling the woman she can quit anytime she chooses. Naturally, the woman often does as the crowd suggests and quits to spend more time with her family, or to start one. This is the point, she says, when women should lean in and not give up. Sandberg received considerable heat from feminists for saying this. They charge that her book stresses individual empowerment too much, that not all women are qualified to reach for the brass ring, and that her view is elitist and fails to address the needs of most women.

But Sandberg has a point, one that is more nuanced than the one she is being criticized for by her detractors. Individual empowerment is essential for moving forward, as she suggests, but for men *and* women. As Sandberg noted, women often give up on their careers when they decide to have children before it is too late. With husbands often making more than them at the early stages of their careers, when they are of child-bearing age, they see the high cost of child care, which their salaries might barely exceed or not cover, and say, "I can stay home and save that money." They see it as an investment in his career and their future earnings.

But what they are not taking into account is the high cost to their careers and the loss of what the woman had invested in her career. In capitalistic terms, her ROI (return on investment) is lost. With women now outpacing men in education, job status, and future potential earnings, walking away from her job makes less sense over the long haul.

Men who run this "marathon" also miss out on their families; they often also end up burnt out at the end of a career, sticking with it even when the love for the job has long since died. Such men often end up so desperately identifying with their careers that once they are forced to retire—or, as happens more often these days, forced out through layoffs and facing job discrimination against hiring older workers—they simply give up. On everything. They sit around the house in pajamas, yelling at the television set, in retirement.

If for no other reason, this new reality of employment forces a shared crown of kingship that not only pays off economically, as couples team for economic well-being, but for social and personal health. Today's economic and social pressures require couples to work together, not only day to day but over the long term, to assess earning capacity, individual preferences, and personality traits.

Raising a family today is more of a shared responsibility than in previous years. With young people, even young marrieds, now living with their parents in order to save money for a home and pay off college debt, the demands of family life are more communal. It might be that the man is better suited in his career to stay at home while his wife toils in the executive suite—or builds her career in management.

Choosing to return to work and leave a child in someone else's care is a difficult decision, Sandberg writes, and one that she agonized over. But it doesn't have to be that way. As Phil Lerman, a TV executive turning 50, learned when he quit his job to take care of his three-year-old, the process of raising a child can be one of the most rewarding experiences of a man's life. His book *Daditude: How a Real Man Became a Real Dad* is entertaining reading. I highly recommend it—not only for men who have had children that they had a hand in raising, for the memories it inspires, but for men contemplating fatherhood, even at an advanced age. Sandberg advises couples to make their partner a real partner when it comes to child rearing. Men need to "lean in" on family life, too. The roles that were considered the norm before 2000 no longer apply.

In fact, as feminist Virginia Woolf outlined in the early 20th century, having child rearing be the sole occupation of women may actually work to the detriment of an equal society. In Woolf's view, women's exclusive charge over infants, without a male sharing the duties, leads to misogynistic tendencies among male children, as it creates an immense need for the love of the mother via breast nourishment and hatred and fear of the mother because of her power and control. The difficulty this sets up for male children to separate from their mothers creates a desire in adult males to dominate and control women.

Woolf felt that when women share mothering duties and give up possessive mothering, their offspring gain a more balanced view of life and male children are acculturated to the idea of child rearing as a shared duty. In her view, this would remove much of the psychic steam propelling oppression of women and would also lead to a more peaceful society, with less war, since it is only through giving up their domination of women that men can stop being tyrants. Woolf asserted that patriarchy encourages men to become slaves to the desire of becoming a dictator.[6]

The scenario of men as sole providers for their families is a recent one. For most of the history of humankind, women also shared in such duties. The idea of the pampered stay-at-home housewife and the scenario where the man went to work and the woman stayed home and raised the kids is a Victorian idea, adopted by the middle class from affluent role models of the 19th century. The assumption was that a man who was successful could afford to "keep" a wife at home who didn't have to work.

Women were reared to accept this living arrangement as proper, and only men who had jobs that paid enough to accomplish it were suitable for marriage. This became the middle class dream, along with home ownership, "a man's home is his castle," and the pursuit of white collar jobs in hierarchical corporations.

This model of marriage gathered steam after World War I, when thousands of men came home from war and left the farm fields behind. It accelerated after World War II, but not until that war also planted the seed of women in the workplace. While the men were off to war, women filled traditional male jobs and found not only that they could do any job as well as men—think of Rosie the Riveter— but that they liked the challenges, the sense of accomplishment, and the independence of a paycheck.

While the 1950s may have been the height of the stereotypical *Leave it to Beaver* home—two parents, with the husband working and wife staying at home—it also saw young women exercising their freedom, liberated by the birth control pill, and reacting against the model they saw in their homes.

The roots of the modern feminist movement may, ironically, be tied to the then-budding tanning industry. Not only did bikinis show women's independence as a result of women choosing to openly display their bodies instead of covering up, but the tan itself was a statement. In the Victorian era, cover-up clothing, including large hats, allowed white women to maintain the whiteness of their skin, showing that they did not do manual labor, thereby making them a cut above tradesmen and women. Even with skin-covering clothing, Victorian women showed their physical shape, and even heightened it through the use of extremely confining girdles and bustles; however, the actual showing of flesh— even something as seemingly innocuous as a bare ankle—was considered scandalously risque.

For much of history, and notably in indigenous cultures throughout the world, men and women have been equal partners in providing food. In hunter-gatherer societies, men hunted and women gathered. Sometimes the bulk of the diet was hunted food, sometimes gathered food, but often a mixture of both. In settled agrarian societies, women worked in fields, as did men; even in modern times on the farm, women usually provided food through kitchen gardens, gathering eggs, milking cows or goats, churning butter, and other chores, in addition to household work, while men performed jobs requiring more muscle power, such as harnessing animals and plowing—though this was by no means universal. The work carried out by individuals on farms varied, as did their roles and daily chores.

Couplehood and Parenthood Are Changing

As noted earlier, couplehood is changing, as is the percentage of young people living alone, as is the number of women having children without marriage.

Cohabitation, or couples living together without marriage, has increased by more than 900 percent in the past 50 years, according to Arielle Kuperberg, sociologist at The University of North Carolina Greensboro.[7]

In a survey of cohabitating couples from 2006 to 2010, about 70 percent of women with less than a high school diploma lived together before marriage, compared to 47 percent of women with a bachelor's degree or higher, according to the Centers for Disease Control and Prevention.

Living together before marriage is a growing trend. In fact, two-thirds of new marriages are between couples who have already lived together for an average of 31 months, according to the research.[8] In fact, for the minority of women who had a higher than average risk of divorcing—women with a premarital birth, women raised in single or stepparent families, or women who had had more than the median number of sex partners—living together while engaged was actually more protective against divorce than moving directly into marriage.

But, while parental and couplehood shifts are occurring, neither males nor females are living the wild life when it comes to sex partners that is often depicted on popular television shows.

According to the U.S. Centers for Disease Control and Prevention, between 2006 and 2012, the median number of female sexual partners in a lifetime for men 25–44 years of age was 6.1. The median number means that as many men had more female sex partners and as many men had fewer, so it's not biased toward the highest and lowest numbers of sex partners (such as someone, say, having 1,000 sex partners skewing the figures), but exactly in the middle, or true average. The percent of men aged 15–44 years of age who have had 15 or more female sexual partners during that same time was 21.6 percent. So, as you can see, most men have only a handful of female sex partners during their most active sex lives.

Between 2006 and 2012, among women aged 25–44 years of age, the median number of male sexual partners was 3.6. During that same time, the percentage of women aged 15–44 years of age who have had 15 or more male sexual partners was 9 percent. So, a few women are having many sex partners, but most have relatively few during their most active years sexually.

The emerging trend of couples sharing duties in child rearing and household chores has positive effects. As Michael Kimmel outlines in *Manhood in America: A Cultural History*, most men have accepted the changes without complaint as a fact of modern life. It's the result of countless micro-decisions made every day. Such decisions include men accepting the dual-career couple as a modern new archetype; being concerned about their male and female children's education; finding harassment and bullying intolerable in any circumstance; understanding wage equality to be a matter of fairness; and growing into the archetype of the new man who finds egalitarian relationships simply a comfortable, rational, and responsible place to be.

Men who practice equality in their relationships have more sex. According to an article in *Men's Health* magazine, with the headline "Housework Makes Her Horny" (meaning: men sharing in the housework!), gender equality in relationships puts less stress on families and leads to happier relations between couples, including in the bedroom.[9]

Men Share the Crown as Authority Figures, Too

One of the hurdles in changing male archetypes is men's insistence on being authority figures, not only when called upon to do so but (and perhaps especially) when it is inappropriate. In feminist philosophy, this trait has been given the moniker of "mansplaining," that men feel compelled to give their opinions as authoritative, even on matters that are intimate to women among women, including matters of sex, personal contraception, social relations, and other issues. (For more on this, see the writings of Rebecca Solnit and her book of essays, *Men Explain Things to Me*.)

This trait is not merely an irritating quality among men (some might say that women, particularly wives, mirror the activity), but has deeper roots in Western society itself. Since the overthrow of the goddess cultures, some three millennia ago, the thrust of society has been to groom men to become leaders from childhood; indeed, more than women, men have been expected to be leaders, with the psychological and sociological underpinnings of society supporting that belief, with all its accompanying inertia.

As social psychologist Jonathan Haidt's research has shown, the psychology of morality, or what people hold to be true and just, is not arrived at by rational choices but by gut feelings and group consensus. Inbred into humans is what Haidt euphemistically calls a "morality gene," whereby humans seek cooperation. That is how our species evolved.

The problem is that while humans want to cooperate, they process information on an issue and then unite to form groups of like-minded folks that each contend is more moral than the other. While it may seem obvious, the conservative ideology that views patriarchy as ground truth, and which holds sway among the elites that determine money, status and power, equates authority with morality. This is the critical characteristic in this discussion—and in society as a whole.

On the other hand, contends Haidt, liberals do not equate authority with morality. Hence, those who hold views that are considered liberal—such as rejecting gender bias and questioning gender roles—do not see those views as immoral, in the same way that conservatives do. The equation of authority with morality may be used to justify extreme views and passions directed at those who reject the conservative view of social order, and reinforces adherence to that view, even as rational and empirical evidence about the changing roles of women demand a new perspective.[10]

In order to address changing roles in modern society, what is needed is an iconoclastic way of viewing the world, one that reaches beyond the dichotomy of liberal/conservative. This may be one reason why modern politics is so divisive, seemingly not amenable to cordial debate to find common ground. Economic disparities are becoming too glaring, while traditional gender roles are failing, and the new reality of common life no longer fits traditional, conservative categories. The stay-at-home housewife mom of the 1950s is now a CEO, worried about her stock portfolio, while dear old Dad is demanding public baby diaper changing tables and flextime at the workplace to take care of junior.

Who's the liberal here, and who's the conservative? The consensus of politicians: focus on splinter groups and hot-button issues, and avoid any substantive debate that would tend to blur the issues.

This blind eye toward the views of others is an externalization of the numbness men have regarding their feelings. Male children are raised from birth not to be "sissies" like women, to not feel or emote. We are all victims of war, as we rob half of our youth of their ability to feel and the other half become willing enablers of this dysfunction, in order to provide infantry, or emotional infants in men's bodies for the giant war machine.

In order to turn around this insensitivity toward self and others, we must encourage young men to feel, experience, and say what they feel. Doing "manly things" is a conscious choice, whether that means to cry or maintain a brave face, whether to share or keep silent. These are choices in the moment; they are not overriding ways of being. That disconnect leads men to become angry, bitter, and abusive— men who are likely to keel over from a heart attack, as a result of needing to maintain a mask on the outside while inside they experience exhortations that the heart reads as bitter grief and sorrow.

Guilt. Shame. A feeling of artificial virility. Toughness. These are the competing emotions that tear at a man in middle age, as he sees his life being wasted in submission to others' ideals, trapped in a life not of his own making or satisfaction, but unable to break free and find what makes him happy out of obligations to others and a social/political system that requires him to fit a mold. We must create for young men the idea that it's okay to be a hero and to carve a hero's path that includes the greatest quest of all: discovery of self. It's okay to cry, to laugh, to grieve, to explore, to shamelessly act the fool, and to learn to be wise through seeing mistakes not as worthy of punishment but as creative opportunities to grow.

Ancient Knowledge Gives Guidance

People speak a great deal about the "ancient knowledge" that can be used to guide us, frequently referring to the Egyptians, Greeks, and the Aztec and Mayan cultures of the Americas. Christ was born more than 2,000 years ago. The classical period of Greece started around 480 BC. Buddha, Siddhartha Gautama, was born around 563 BC. The Great Pyramid in Egypt was built around 2550 BC. The Mayan calendar begins around 3114 BC. The oldest parts of the Bible refer to the times of Enoch and the prophet Elijah, during the time of the Sumerians, around 3500 BC. So, the oldest of these sources are 5,000–6,000 years old.

The salient point is that male patriarchy has only been around about 2,000 years, since the time of the Romans. Before that, matriarchal societies oversaw much of the conduct of humanity—a state that continued in various degrees in the Americas until Europeans came.

For most of the history of humankind, long before the rise of Islam, Christianity, and Buddhism, societies were more balanced. And, in fact, the early teachings of each of those religions were more balanced than many of the current teachings regarding the roles of women and men. Traditional Native American societies may be the best models of balanced societies in existence today—with only about 500 years of European contact and assimilation, versus 2,000 years.

In Native society, an important point for this discussion is how Native people viewed themselves—not their political, social, or religious lives—but as individuals. Without exception, the names that Native groups gave themselves generally translated to "the People" or "human beings." (Many of the names now given tribes that are recognized by the federal government were ascribed to them by others, frequently their enemies.)

This marks an important aspect of community since it declares each person in the group to have worth as a human being—not as an object or an affiliation (such as a nation-state or ethnic division) but as one of all beings who are human. As a human being, a person has an important distinction: personhood. Along with that distinction, it is understood that everyone starts off equal.[11]

Since every issue has a yang as well as a yin, some have noted that this insistence has a down side for tribes (or, more accurately, bands, moieties, or family groups, since "tribe" is a European concept imposed on Native Americans so that the government could obtain treaties and land rights). That down side is the very notion of tribalism: that one group is composed of "human beings" while another group is not.

In the absence of any view to the contrary, this would seem to be the case; however, in practice, Native groups were very aware of other groups. They even expressed kinship with many of them—for example, claiming a stronger group to be an "uncle" or another to be a "cousin." Other groupings, even at war, were considered to be "relations." They might be seen as not right in the head, or bewitched, or led in a bad way, but they were relations, nonetheless.

Modern tribes are designated as tribes because they speak, or spoke, the same language or a dialect; however, prior to European conquest, that didn't mean that all who spoke one language got along. Some groupings had spun off from others hundreds, even a thousand, years before.

For example, today's Choctaws, or those allied to them through language, lived in Texas, Louisiana, Mississippi, Alabama, Georgia, and Florida, but were made up of hundreds of moieties. (The Choctaw language—variants of Muskogean—was often used as a trade language that united many small bands.) Because of fears over inbreeding, it was common for people to marry outside the tribe. The proscription, however, had a socializing effect beyond the immediate tribe: clans denoted by totems such as wolf, bear, eagle, and the like were shared among far-off relations. They could be counted on to watch over and protect travelers who came hunting or on missions of trade and for gatherings. So, social interaction in peaceful ways was guaranteed over hundreds of miles and often enforced through kinship.

Often, it was said with respect that a person—man or woman—who exemplified ideals of wisdom, courage, leadership, self-sacrifice, and compassion for his or her people, was "a real human being." Being a human being carried responsibilities that transcended roles, distinctions, clan affiliations, and other duties.

One of my favorite books is *Profiles in Wisdom: Native Elders Speak About the Earth* by Steven McFadden. In it, he interviews Native people about who they are, how they are coexisting with this society, and they offer a great deal of wisdom, much of it handed down.

In one of the stories, a woman talks about her childhood and how, because she was reared in the Native way, she received the great gift of self-esteem. It was a great gift because of the hardship she had to endure once she was an adult and trying to make her way in the world. In one telling instance, she talks about how she coped, and how her self-esteem, instilled since childhood, kept her strong. The secret? Although she was raised Catholic, it was the circle of love provided by her family that acted as a mirror to form her early views of herself. "I don't consider myself an Indian or non-Indian or anything else," she said. "I consider myself a human being." With that understanding, all the prejudice and hate she encountered fell away, since those were simply the failures of other human beings.

As stated in *To Become a Human Being: The Message of Tadodaho Chief Leon Shenandoah* by Steve Wall, "There's no such thing as Indian. Just 'Human Being.'" If we are going to start anew with our archetypes, then, what better way to determine the qualities of being that matter than those of being a human being. Traditionally recognized Native traits include:

GENEROSITY: There was no greater way to build status in Native communities than to show generosity, especially for those who could not provide for themselves. Good hunters gave food to elders and families in need. Those who excelled at craftwork might exchange their bounty with the bounty of others. In some Native societies, such as those in the Northwest who practiced the Potlatch, or pot-luck, the amount that one could give away was a mark of wealth.[12] The tradition of the "giveaway" continues today, wherever traditional ceremonies are held, when every individual who attends, regardless of social status, is given something.

FORGIVENESS: Traditionally, giveaway is also practiced when one is wronged. You give the person who slighted you a gift so that you do not carry that hurt or pain. You give it away. It shows you are not harmed; it keeps you in balance and allows you to forget the slight. Why live with someone else's rudeness? It also allows the other person to "wake up" and see that there is no wrong intended, allowing an opportunity for reconciliation. The goal is to bring yourself and all around you into balance, and to heal whatever is wrong. If the rift continues, it doesn't belong to you—allowing you to walk away, without anger—a step beyond turning the other cheek.

SACREDNESS: Native people recognized that human beings only walked the earth for a limited time; all things, material and immaterial, were sacred. The Creator was bigger than human beings could comprehend and, hence, was sometimes called "The Great Mystery." When a human being was balanced, he or she was poised between Heaven and Earth, a child of the Creator, co-creating. Walking in balance was to appreciate miracles all around, all the time: above and below, before and behind, inside. To appreciate this sacred harmony was to Walk in Beauty. At heart, someone who is a human being is someone who is spiritually connected. All else radiates from this.

SHARING: In Native society, all beings were considered "relations." When one killed to eat, for example, a prayer was said over the animal that was killed to thank it for its sacrifice. This was also done when choosing plants to eat. When picking berries or leaves for food, one didn't strip the plant of all its leaves or fruit; some was left so that it could survive and thrive and continue to provide food for other beings and for human beings in the future.

THRIFT AND RESOURCEFULNESS: Native people didn't hoard physical items or gather unnecessary goods ("wealth"). Only items that were to be used were kept; other items were given away to those who needed them. The term "Indian giver," where one takes back what was given, has an element of truth. In Native societies, if someone wasn't using something, it often was taken back and given to someone who could use it—without anger or blame. It was just a facet of tribal life where property is shared for the common good.

EXERCISING HUMAN GOODNESS: Love, spirit, joy, mindfulness, honesty, and compassion.

This way of viewing relationships—from self, to Creator, to Earth, to all beings—reminds us that we as human beings are unique. We are children of Earth and Sky: Earth because all of the elements in our bodies come from the Earth Mother; Sky because our spirits are ethereal and eternal and come from the Creator, Heavenly Father, Maker of All Things.

When we see ourselves as beings who are divine in origin (spiritual beings in human bodies) and designated co-creators upon this earth, then we see ourselves as being in our rightful place, as taking a right relationship with our worldly and spiritual obligations. We are human beings, unique upon the earth, and we share this divinity—and obligation—with all human beings.

When we walk in beauty, in right relationship with Heaven and Earth, then the madness and insanity of the dysfunction of society falls away. It becomes a separate thing, something to walk through but not be a part of, and we can see other human beings—those who act with love, spirit, joy, mindfulness, honesty, and compassion—as transcending the sickness that surrounds us all. They have their own reality, their own luminosity, their own characteristics that come through not only in their words and deeds but in their presence that marks them as real human beings.

Mars? Venus? Women are from Earth, Men are from Earth

Contrary to certain popular books, as a human being, you cannot see women (or men) as being from another planet. In future years, historians will look back upon this time and wonder: how did anybody get along with such divisiveness?   To be fair, John Gray's books, such as *Men are From Mars, Women Are From Venus*, are excellent, perceptive guides toward male/female relationships; however, while the substance of the books is instructive, sensitive, and caring, the catchy title leads to the false impression that men and women are intrinsically unalike, are predisposed toward conflict with one another, and unable to find common ground. It promotes the stereotype of the war of the sexes, a competition, with the underlying belief that there is only one winner and one loser, and may the stronger prevail.

This competitiveness affects not only men and women but society as a whole. We have people in our legislatures who not only do not listen to people with opposing points of view but refuse to entertain any notions of compromise. Some partisans would rather bring down the whole government than compromise, despite all the pain and suffering that this would cause millions of sick, unemployed, very young, and very elderly people whose lives depend on assistance. Many Christian churches view Christians not of their denomination as "going to hell." And some Muslim sects have deadly feuds lasting generations. Our lives are filled with division.

When the whole thrust of society seems to be highlighting differences rather than similarities and shared goals, it's no wonder people with differing views cannot speak civilly to each other and come to agreements. And here, because of a popular book a few years ago, half of the human race is being relegated as being alien because men and women have different views on issues of importance to them?

It's true that polls show men and women generally view issues differently. The Republican Party in America, for example, is decidedly white and male. But that doesn't mean that men and women don't share values and concerns of vital interest to them in significantly important ways.

The point is that men and women should see each other as, first, human beings who share values and ideals. They can participate in a dialogue with one another to determine those ideals, then work together to achieve mutual goals. Of themselves, differences are not detrimental; indeed, it's useful to get the whole story. People with different views and ways of processing information can weave their own tapestries of understanding that are much stronger than a one-sided or dictated view.

The danger of viewing women as a separate race of beings, as happened with the rise of patriarchies, is that it destroys the fabric of society. Children should be secure in the belief that their parents matter, children matter, that human beings matter. They should rest secure in the nurturing knowledge that love, spirit, joy, mindfulness, honesty, and compassion are the foundation stones upon which human beings base their understandings—and that transcends gender, race, or any other distinction.

When it comes to teaching guiding principles, we need a different way. The concepts (ideals) of kingship and discipleship are outwardly defined and, ultimately, unattainable, and the impossible standards for being a lover or a warrior are not defined by what matters in the moment. A better way may be to harken back to the Native American model of having an "informed heart." When your world is defined by who you really are—the silence between the voices in your mind, or the person who hears those voices—rather than the voices of those telling you who you are or should be, then you will be on the right path.

Cultivating this "one who hears and acts" then becomes a way of deciding our approach—be it king, lover, warrior, or magician—because the heart encompasses all these attributes and a myriad of others: child, man, masculine, feminine, sage, fool, and more. Why limit yourself to a handful of rarely useful ways of being when you hold within you a full range of behaviors and relationships, many untried and some uniquely your own? Why play out moribund roles when each moment offers opportunities to live and love as a unique human being unrestricted by the narrow thoughts and beliefs of others you might not even know, much less care to honor or respect?

As men, we have that opportunity: to seek to know ourselves and, hence, to bring rich resources of love, respect, wisdom, and compassion to all within our sacred circles. This is not the "end of men" but the beginning of manhood redefined.

EXERCISE 1: *Inventory Your Inner Relationship Goals*

What male qualities would you ascribe as necessary to being a real human being?
- Good husband, parent, father, friend?
- Provider for yourself and loved ones?
- Source of spiritual guidance and joy?
- Role model for young people—your children and others?

Make of list of qualities you fill, and those that you desire to fill. Some would be: leadership, reliability, truth in words and deeds. Who do you know, in fact or fiction, who fulfills these qualities? This becomes a list of your personal archetypes.

EXERCISE 2: *List the Joys of Being a Man*

Make a list of experiences that you consider part of being a man, and how they make you feel.
The list might include:
- Having strong muscles, feeling them flex, working out, and knowing that I feel and look manly;
- Being with other men, their banter, the camaraderie of joking and subtle insults that define a masculine relationship between men;
- Waking up with an erection in the morning;

- Holding your child and feeling the love, trust, and fragility of that little being;
- Enjoying the company of your son, feeling in awe and proud of him that he has become his own person;
- Giving your daughter away in marriage, and knowing that you will always be her daddy.

These are just a few examples. Your list may be entirely different. There are no wrong answers—only answers that make you the type of man you are. If you are inclined, share them with significant others in your family and friendship circles and see how they compare.

EXERCISE 3: *Perceive Human Beings*

Walk into any room full of people, whether it's a loose association, such as a restaurant, or a business meeting, a school classroom, or a cocktail party, and dispassionately view the people there. Open up your sensing ability; see with your feelings, not merely your eyes. Look for human beings.

Allow those who are exhibiting the qualities of love, spirit, joy, mindfulness, honesty, and compassion to come forward in your consciousness. Slowly, one by one, your attention will be drawn here or there, to a person in the corner, or another reading a book, another smiling and talking to someone, and so on. Individuals will stand out with their luminosity.

Merely by setting your intent, you will begin to see people who have their own energy, their own gravitas, that sets them apart. They will either be excited and passionate, or quiet and reserved, or listening or talking, or any combination; but if you focus on looking for "human beings," those who have heart and soul, not those who are unconscious or existing superficially, will appear, even in a large group of people, as human beings, separate and distinct.

For more on assessing the energy of people, places, and things, see my book *Clearing: A Guide to Liberating Energy Trapped in Buildings and Lands*. The relationship between people and their environments can be profound. Reading the energy of people, places, and things can help propel you to new realities.

EXERCISE 4: *Recalibrating Attachment to Objects and Activities*

A positive way of assessing where you are in your relationship with objects and activities that define who you are is to take an inventory of the objects and activities that take up your time.

By reassessing what holds value for you, how that has changed over time, and what you believe may hold greater interest, you may be able to help yourself evolve into a new way of being. Only by assessing where we are and where we have come from are we able to determine where we want to be.

Make a list of objects and activities you enjoy or have enjoyed, in no particular order. Examples might include:

- Guns
- Knives
- Cars
- Tools
- Clothes
- Sports Equipment
- Cigars
- Alcoholic Beverages—martinis, mimosas, gin and tonics, beer, etc.
- Dancing
- Dining
- Sex
- Art
- Music
- Fishing
- Hunting
- Boating
- Boots
- Reading
- Book Collecting
- Spiritual Retreats
- Dating
- Hang Gliding
- Rock Climbing
- Caving
- Surfing
- Swimming
- Fossil Hunting
- Horseback Riding

You get the idea. Make a list, then see how your interests have changed. Write in your journal how the person who did these activities in the past changed to other activities and why. What specific events occurred to stimulate interest and what events changed or ended them? Detail the significant events, such as first sexual encounter. What do you remember about it? How did it affect your views about sex and your partner? Do you still approach sex in the same way? Is it appropriate? How did your views change? Why did they change? Is it time to reassess and base your behavior in another way? How should you go about it?

Create a "bucket list" of achievable changes in objects and activities. For example, you have listed travel and determined that you traveled extensively at one period in your life, but for some reason, you stopped. What stopped you? Are there places you would still like to go? List them. Put them on a list of things to do.

In dining, for example, have you approached food as a gourmand, savoring the foods prepared for you? Or has food been just mass quantities of protein and vegetable matter to fuel your body. Is that something you wish to change? How would you go about it? Are there people in your life who can help you? Are there books, magazines, YouTube videos, and websites that you can Google to find out more? Put it in your list in your journal of things to do. Don't be too judgmental. Experience, grow, evolve!

For example, although I quit smoking years ago, I've been experimenting with fine cigars. I limit myself to no more than one per day, and often one per week. I love hand rolled because of the craftsmanship involved. Luckily, there is a man named Felix, a native of Cuba and true *toquero* from whom I buy locally. It's an honorable tradition where he comes from, and exploring the taste sensations of fine cigars has added to my appreciation of food. Personally, I like the darker, spicier wrappers—*Habano, Meduro, Oscuro*, and for special occasions and when I can find them, *Rosado*. My favorite commercially available hand rolled is the *La Gloria Cubana Artesanos de Tabaqueros Toro*. I enjoy it for its bold blend that still keeps smooth. For me, a cigar is like a dessert, a special treat. Just as you wouldn't want to eat ice cream and cake too often, so it is with a fine cigar. As time goes on, I suspect my interest in this will change, too.

This inventory is to help you evolve, shift, change, enliven, and broaden your life, and help you become the person you can be while you are on this Earth School.

Make the intention to change. By simply intending to change, your attention will change, you will find the people, places, and things that will help you change. You will find that your energetic attachments will unconsciously shift. You may feel your assemblage points (energy in the solar plexus region) churn to bring new experiences and realities into your life. You will change, and your world and your reality will change.

Share your list with your significant other, if you desire that person to accompany you in your changing reality. Be aware, however, that often we attach to objects and behaviors not because we want them, but because we have come to accept them as part of our partner's way of being.

If you find that your significant other has a different set of objects and behaviors that are drawing him/her, then you must honestly face that fact. If that is the case, then you must decide if you want to continue along the path that is being set for you by these attachments, or if you want to pursue your own goals and needs.

A way to determine if your goals and needs are shared, if your relationship with your significant other is moving you forward or holding you back, is to inventory those shared and different objects and behaviors.

Take your journal and make three lists. Start with shared objects and behaviors such as: home, leisure pursuits, interests, hobbies, attitudes, and so on. Then, list those items that belong to you alone, and then those that belong to the other alone.

You may find that most of the activities either belong to you or to the other. That's fine, if you and the other are happy with it. But you may also find that a lot of your pursuits, objects, and interests really belong to the other person; you have adopted them as your own, yet find no great pleasure in them. You may find that you have left behind the pursuits, objects, and interests that once belonged to you, and that you miss them. Or you may find that those old interests have been adopted by the other, and that you no longer find pleasure in them.

By gentle questioning of your significant other, you may find that you both are pursuing objects and interests that no longer hold value or interest to you both, but you have done so to accommodate the other.

Doing this inventory can be a great way to open a dialogue with your significant other about the status of your relationship and its future. But beware, once this dialogue has begun, it can lead either to greater enrichment or sharing, and/or meaningful change, or to dissolution of the relationship.

EXERCISE 5: *Seeing the Creator in Everything*

In all the great religions, including early Christianity, and among indigenous peoples around the world, a universal belief exists that the Creator's spark, or the divine, lives within all beings.

As an exercise, sit in a quiet place and still the inner clamor until a level of repose is reached. Don't force thoughts from your mind, as in doing so, they frequently come back even louder for the attempt; simply brush them aside. Keep your intent on maintaining quiet, calm, and openness.

Once that level is reached, imagine that all things around you contain the spark of the Creator. In Cherokee belief, *nvwati*, or Spirit (or the good medicine) lives in everything. In Hindu belief, the Sanskrit greeting *namaste* recognizes that the light in me greets the light, or divinity, within you. In the Gospel of Thomas, a Gnostic text, this idea is embodied in some 114 quotes from Jesus, including: "I am the light that shines over all things. I am everything. From me all came forth, and to me all return. Split a piece of wood, and I am there. Lift a stone, and you will find me there." The Essenes, likewise, called themselves Sons of Light, and referred to Psalms 82: "I have said, Ye are gods (*elohim*); and all of you children of the most High (*oliun*)." We are all Children of Heaven and Earth.

Imagine this light in everything you see and hear, touch and imagine. Think of this light as constantly around you, the very epitome of love, compassion, wisdom, and guidance, and emanating from a wise spiritual being of all-encompassing love.

FROM THE AUTHOR'S NOTEBOOK

ON FATHERHOOD

I'M CONSTANTLY AMAZED by the events my son remembers and how some of those memories ricochet through to the life of my grandson.

For example, I was talking to my son, Ross, on the phone and he said that he had taken his son to his first day of school. Ross said it was a poignant moment, knowing that his son was no longer an infant and how hard it was to entrust him to the care of others.

I said that I well remembered taking Ross to school, first to a nursery school, then to a preschool, and especially the first day he had gone alone by himself. He begged me to allow him to leave the car and run in on his own "like the big boys," instead of me walking him in and entrusting him to the caregivers. Finally, I relented. He eagerly grabbed his backpack and ran from the car, slamming the door behind him. I saw him speed across the lawn and enter the building with nary a look back.

It broke my heart. I knew he was no longer my baby but a boy, and he had left on his own separate fate. From here on out, we would truly be two people, with different experiences, different walks in the world, independent of each other, bound by an ever more tenuous tie until finally we would only speak by phone, every once in a while, or a lunch here and there, as with my father before me. He had just taken the first step toward manhood—eagerly, without hesitation and without looking back.

As I was musing on this, Ross broke my reverie by sharing that when he dropped his son Nathan off at nursery school, he noticed that his car radio was on National Public Radio, as it had been when he was a child, with the same drone of international events as when I had dropped him off at nursery school a quarter of a century before. This time, the crisis was in Syria rather than Bosnia, he noted, but the reportage was the same: tragedy, war, disrupted lives, barbarity, genocide, all the great evils of human kind related in droll monotone, the drumbeat of our lives in constant war.

That made me shudder. I recalled that when George W. Bush announced his war plans, I feared for my son, that he would be drafted, taken from me, killed or maimed, my only son. I had known friends whose brothers did not return from Vietnam or who had come back crippled, physically or emotionally, and never recovered.

I thought of Bush. Damn these politicians! When will the bloodletting stop? For what purpose do we sacrifice our sons and fathers, brothers and uncles in this constant killing machine? So the multinational corporations can claim more profits? Whether it's oil in the Mideast, tin in Indochina, or bananas in the Caribbean, where does it stop?

It's a chilling thought—the generations bound by love, loss, and growing, with a backdrop of war. This is the story of modern manhood? The distinction perhaps being how close to the killing we actually may be? Let's work toward a path of peace—of being men of wisdom, not reaction, of carving our own paths of freedom, in which war is only the last resort not the first option.

If we can harness the great forces of egalitarianism that have been gaining momentum over the past 300 years, and embrace the participation of all people regardless of gender, shucking the worst excesses of patriarchy toward a more perfect and balanced union, we can achieve peace and prosperity. We can create a society, like the Iroquois and other Native peoples, who recognized the importance of working for the whole people, all human beings, rather than just a few. This future can release us from the constant bondage of war, killing, genocide, and tyranny.

For us men, it starts with being a man. Teaching our sons that war and violence, whether it be toward women, other men, or those who are different, is not an achievement; it is a failure—a failure of reasoning, cooperation, finding common goals with a commitment toward securing a better life for ourselves and succeeding generations, not short-term gain. We are hunters of the best and highest good—for self, others, the Creator, for all human beings—not killers bent on annihilation.

Let's unleash our children upon the world with a brighter path, and let their eagerness take them to a better life, a better world, with nary a look back.

FROM THE AUTHOR'S NOTEBOOK

BEING A HUMAN BEING USING 12-STEP PROGRAMS

PROBABLY NO OTHER PROGRAM has been more successful at changing people's lives and behavior for the good than Alcoholics Anonymous. Its tenets have been copied and adapted to every type of behavior, from binge eating to sex addiction. It also shares a key element in changing one's motivations and outlook by how one views self and others.

In *The Big Book of Alcoholics Anonymous*, it says, "We have begun to learn tolerance, patience and good will toward all men, even our enemies, for we look on them as sick people." The purpose of this philosophy is to see that much (perhaps most) of social behavior can be considered perverse or not aimed at individual health, social and emotional progress, or highest good for self or society. Indeed, much of average life is contrary to the personal wellness and best interests of the individual, and instead promotes values that favor special interests, entrenched elites, or institutions.

For example, an employee may constantly be held accountable for the failures of a business—their hours, job duties, and very livelihood depend on it. But as AA sessions point out, a system where a person is held accountable for actions over which he or she has no control is dysfunctional: you can only be held accountable for your own behavior. Conversely, unnecessary worry over someone else's actions, beliefs, or thoughts is dysfunctional. It's a sick way of viewing the world. If adopted by the alcoholic, both forms of dysfunction can be dangerous triggers for building resentments toward workplace, friends, loved ones, family, and others, and it can lead to a return to drinking as a solution for such dysfunction.

The solution, though, is not to condemn these systems, but to accept them for what they are without personal attachment. As AA's trademark Serenity Prayer outlines: "God grant me the serenity to accept the things I cannot change; the courage to change the things I can; and the wisdom to know the difference." This requires an objectivity, discernment, and judgment that distances the recovering alcoholic from those around him or her, and even from the society he or she must live within. It is the same with defining oneself as a human being—a person capable of thought, discernment, judgment, and behavior that recognizes others like oneself and rejects people, places, and things that are not fit for human beings.

In the traditional Native way, one can only look at certain Western practices and see them as symptoms of sickness. It's well understood that Native people thought the first Europeans were crazy, or not human beings. How could one "own" the earth? The sky? The land? Of course, now we have corporations that say they own huge tracts of land and are entitled to despoil it any way they wish. We have elites that say they not only own the dwellings and buildings but the air rights that extend upwards, the mineral rights below, even where other people have built their houses and live daily lives, and the water rights that flow to it, even hundreds of miles away.

Native people "counted coup" on enemies. Instead of killing them, the mark of a brave warrior was to confront and touch the other person in battle and show no fear, displaying that he could have killed the other, but didn't. Who is the greater warrior? One who chooses life, or one who chooses death? To kill without personal responsibility was shameful.

In modern war, we use unmanned drones without shame or remorse or personal responsibility, even when they have been documented to inadvertently and repeatedly wipe out innocent civilians.

In my opinion, a human being would not use a drone to kill someone—much less men, women, and children, sight unseen. A human being would not lay claim to vast lands over which he or she has no use but to own it, and keep others away so that they cannot enjoy it. A human being would not buy air, water, or minerals beneath another person's feet and deny that person access to it. A human being would look at humanity and see other human beings—not numbers or clients or people able to be duped or taken advantage of in impersonal schemes.

As William Griffith Wilson (or simply "Bill," the founder of AA) said, the great killers of a life built on spirituality (and, hence, sobriety) are selfishness, dishonesty, resentment, and fear.

If you are at your core a hunter—not a warrior, but someone who seeks nourishment and provisions for self and others—look out for these traits in yourself in order to resolve them. You can keep on a path of wisdom and compassion. This is what Yaqui shaman Don Juan Matus meant when he said we must learn to stalk ourselves, our own peccadilloes. It is at the core of being a man of knowledge.

If you can stay on a path of balance and sobriety—that is, truly seeing what is around you and how it reflects your world within—you will become a maker of miracles. The greatest of those miracles will be the re-creation or redefinition of your self. You will become a true human being and your own archetype of manhood in your relationship with others.

Brother Bill of AA had it right: Much of what passes for modern life is a disease. The choice we each have is whether we allow it to infect us, our families and children, and pass it on. Or if we say: It stops here. I'm a human being, and I will act like one, even if I'm surrounded by sickness.

That is the choice we each must make.

Review

New archetypes, behaviors, and models for a new world:

- Recognize old archetypical behaviors, and the new replacement behaviors that are emerging, as seen, for example, in the contrast in alternatives offered by U.S. Presidents George W. Bush (the old dominator model) and the more inclusive Barack Obama.

- Notice that loner archetypes found in popular culture and fiction, such as detective novels, Westerns, and macho "revenge" films may have lofty goals but still rely on violence and projection of power to achieve ends, highlighting the inequities of patriarchal culture.

- Observe that while traditional families are disintegrating, new forms of family are emerging, with Native American and historical indigenous cultures providing positive role models individually and collectively.

- Revel in the new relationships available to men through shared sexual intimacy, the joint rearing of children, and helping young people and significant others in their development, as well as yourself, physically, emotionally, spiritually.

- Recognize that the female principle gives life; the male principle gives direction and purpose. Each has its way of being, and neither could exist without the other. They are different but equal.

- Rejoice in the fact that being a human being, sharing the best qualities of manhood, personhood, and local and global citizenship is a real possibility— an archetype we can all share with love, compassion, and goodness.

INTERNET KEY WORDS: *role of the "uncle" in native society, new tribalism, third gender, orenda.*

Glossary

all-time, no-time. The present, accessed at its deepest level.

angels. Emissaries of light of divine origin that accompany humans through life and are available for assistance and inspiration.

animus. The spark of life.

apprehend. In the shamanic way of viewing, to take hold of, arrest, or seize, as perception in an act of understanding, in the moment, without judgment or projection of consciousness.

archetypes. Attributes existing in potential form that can be brought into manifestation; original models after which other similar things are patterned.

assemblage points. Areas in the energy body that "connect" us to what we perceive as reality, both with our senses and beyond our senses, to ground us into a reality we can perceive and understand.

aura. Emanations of the energy body, often seen as colors that show moods, thoughts, or potentials; energetic fields surrounding the physical body, including physical, etheric, emotional, mental, astral, etheric template, celestial, and causal.

authentic self. Who you really are, not who you think you are, or have been told you are by outside sources.

cleansing. Transmuting energy to a higher, more positive form by raising its vibrational rate.

centering. Locating the core of consciousness in the body; drawing magnetic energy from the earth and electrical energy from the sun to operate with balanced awareness.

chakra. Sanskrit for "circle" or "wheel." In Indian Hindu thinking, the energetic centers in the core of the body are linked together by a central psychic energy channel.

clearing. Dissipating (transmuting) negative energy. Clearing spaces usually also cleanses them, since the act of clearing raises the vibrational rate.

Deganawidah. The Peacemaker, a man who brought order and peace to the Iroquois nations.

ego. The survival mechanism, which is part of the personality. See Personality.

energy. Subtle power manifested through life force, frequency, or cohesion.

energy body. A body that exists beyond the physical plane; in humans, such a body extends 27 feet in each direction, and thereafter continues into other dimensions. See Aura.

fast. See Vision quest.

flow of creation. The movement or stasis of energy in a given moment.

God vs. Creator. God is one, all; the Creator is the active aspect of God as expressed in the will of creation.

goddesses. Land spirits of the highest order, usually associated with a place or characteristic; also, humans who have transcended but chosen to remain on Earth in spirit form as a means of service.

grounding. Connecting with the earth energetically to ensure that consciousness is not operating from other dimensions or overly affected by other energetic forces.

guides. Spirit helpers, soul brothers or sisters from former or future lifetimes, or spiritual masters who have assumed a supportive role for a particular soul's evolution.

Haudenosaunee. Indigenous name of the Iroquois tribe.

heart song, or **power song.** A song that expresses the unique, positive energies, traits, and intents of an individual, usually discovered through fasting and prayer.

higher power. God as expressed through one's highest nature.

life-force energy. Energy that is all around us in nature and that is emitted by the earth.

light body. Energetic body; the quality of energy around a person, as opposed to their physical body.

mansplaining. The phenomenon of men feeling compelled to give their opinions to women as authoritative on all issues, with or without expertise, even on matters that are intimate to women among women.

matter. Patterns of energy we perceive as having substance.

medicine. The inherent power within all things.

medicine wheel. A Native American system of prayer, meditation, and discovery that recognizes that life follows a circle. The wheel's directions and their significance, concepts from which all things are said to derive, include east (newness, discovery), south (youth, growth, healing), west (introspection, setting sun, light within), north (wisdom, elders, ancestors), center (soul, spirit), above (Heavenly Father), and below (Earth Mother).

mind of God. Expansion of human thought to higher consciousness as far as is conceivable.

moiety. A tribal subdivision or kinship group; often based on common ancestor; may be grouped as a society, or other distinguishing or self-proclaimed characteristic, with participation through kinship or voluntary association.

native peoples. Indigenous cultures practicing traditional nature-based ways.

new tribalism. Belief that social families are emerging by choice and common interest.

nonordinary reality. Reality as seen when everyday constraints and predispositions are eliminated through trance or other methods.

orenda. Spiritual power; power that is greater than any individual or any society

personality. All that we adhere to, or believe, that makes us who we think we are. See Ego.

pipe fast. See Vision quest.

power animal. An animal that offers guidance and protection; a totem.

prayer stick. A stick, either ornate or plain, that has been consecrated through prayer, wrapped with cloth, ribbon, or yarn, and most often, planted in the ground to carry a prayer.

recapitulation. A shamanic practice in which individuals revisit past experiences to shift perceptions and draw new lessons.

Reiki. A Japanese form of energy medicine involving sacred symbols and guides; use of the hands to channel healing energy.

sacred circle. All beings in our lives—past, present, and future—who are connected to us; consecrated circle for ceremony.

self-talk. The inner dialogue inside our minds; the "what ifs," "buts," judgments, and fears that prevent us from being who we really are.

shaman. Siberian word meaning "one who sees in the dark"; a person who uses earth energy, guides, and power animals for insight; a medicine man or woman.

shielding. Creating, through intent, a protective energy layer around you to deflect external negative energy.

smudging. Burning a plant such as sage, cedar, or sweetgrass to purify the energy of an area; or using liquid smudge derived from plant essences; or using leaves, wood, or plants.

soul. The essential life force, or essence, of a being that is eternal from lifetime to lifetime.

soul retrieval. The act of retrieving soul parts, or essence, lost through trauma or stolen by another individual.

space. Any defined area, including the objects within it.

spiral of ascension. Spiral of life that offers a changing perspective as new lessons are encountered and old ones repeated, until the lessons are finally learned.

spirit. The essential quality of a being as an expression of soul; noncorporeal aspect of a person aligned their with soul purpose.

spirit quest. Following only what spirit dictates, usually over the course of days.

stillpoint. An inner place of total silence and stillness, where intuition and creativity originate and balance can be found; the source of being.

sweat lodge. Sacred enclosed space incorporating energy from heated rocks released as steam as water is poured on them; part of a sacred system including the lodge, a sacred fire, the path between them; ritual space incorporating Native American prayers.

transmutation. Changing energy from one state to another, such as transforming water to ice or vapor and vice versa; changing negative, or inert, energy into positive, or active, energy; or neutralizing energy to be reabsorbed by the earth. Ancient practices involved burying an energized object in the ground, burning it with fire, or submerging it in water.

true face. The face that is open and shows one's true inner nature.

vibrational rate/vibrational frequency. The measurable level of energy of a person, place, or object; the higher the rate, the closer to the source, or optimal wholeness.

vision quest. A period of time spent in a desolate or isolated spot under the tutelage of a spiritual elder, intended as an opportunity for discovering the inner self, the meaning of life, or to connect with higher beings.

will of creation. Energy of the moment, moving from one state to another; the potential to transform to another manifestation.

End Notes

CHAPTER 1

1. For a complete treatment of these and other spiritual techniques, see the author's books *Finding Sanctuary in Nature: Simple Ceremonies in the Native American Tradition* and *Healing Plants and Animals From a Distance: Curative Principles and Applications.*

2. For more on this, see the author's book *Conscious Food: Sustainable Growing, Spiritual Eating*, which traces the loss of female power and influence since the birth of agriculture.

3. Barthes, Roland. *Elements of Semiology*, trans. Annette Lavers and Colin Smith. New York: Hill and Wang, 1967.

4. See www.catalyst.org/knowledge/women-ceos-fortune-1000

5. "An elusive jackpot: riches come to women as C.E.O.s, but few get there." *New York Times*, June 7, 2014.

6. Lerner, Gerder. *The Creation of Patriarchy (Women and History, Vol 1)*. New York: Oxford University Press, 1987.

7. Trebay, Guy. "America's message: At ease, men. American menswear sends a casual message to the world." *The New York Times*, Aug. 20, 2014

8. Chomsky, Noam. "Cuban missile crisis: How the U.S. played Russian roulette with nuclear war." *The Guardian*, Oct. 15, 2012.

CHAPTER 2

1. Robinson, James M., et al. *The Nag Hammadi Library*. New York: HarperSanFrancisco, 1990.

2. McElvaine, Robert S. *Eve's Seed: Biology, the Sexes and the Course of History*. New York: McGraw-Hill, 2000.

3. For more on this, see the author's book *Conscious Food: Sustainable Growing, Spiritual Eating*.

4. Branscombe, Nyla R. and Daniel L. Wann. "The positive social and self concept consequences of sports identification." *Journal of Sport and Social Issues,* September 1991.

5. Messner, Michael A. "Sports and male domination: The female athlete as contested ideological terrain." *University of Southern California, Sociology of Sport Journal,* 1988, Vol. 5.

6. *Thursday Night Football,* CBS TV, Sept. 11, 2014.

7. Kimmel, Michael. *Manhood in America: A Cultural History.* New York: Oxford University Press, 2012.

8. O'Connor, D.B, J. Archer, and F.C. Wu. "Effects of testosterone on mood, aggression, and sexual behavior in young men: a double-blind, placebo-controlled, cross-over study. "*Journal of Endocrinological Metabolism,* June 2004.

9. Seltzer, Leon F. Ph.D. "Evolution of the self: On the paradoxes of personality. "*Psychology Today,* April 28, 2009.

10. Maines, Rachel P. "The Technology of Orgasm: Hysteria" in *The Vibrator, and Women's Sexual Satisfaction.* The Johns Hopkins University Press, 2001.

11. Northrup, Christiane, M.D. *Women's Bodies, Women's Wisdom: Creating Physical and Emotional Health and Healing.* Revised edition. New York: Bantam Books, 2010.

12. Ibid.

13. For more books on energy medicine, see the author's website: *www. blueskywaters.com.*

14. It should be noted that while slavery existed in Native American society, the matriarchal lineage system did not extend to making all women marginalized as property as it did in patriarchal society.

15. For more, see *The Chalice and the Blade* by Riane Eisler. New York: HarperCollins, 1987.

16. For a fascinating walk along this line of reasoning, see "Losing our touch" by Richard Kearney, *The New York Times,* Aug. 31, 2014.

17. Friedman, Thomas L. *The World Is Flat: A Brief History of the Twenty-First Century.* New York: Farrar, Straus and Giroux, 2005.

18. "The Rule of Love: Wife Beating as Prerogative and Privacy" by Reva B. Siegel, *Yale Law School, Faculty Scholarship Series*, Jan. 1, 1996, Yale Law School Legal Scholarship Repository.

19. Thornton, Arland, and L. Young-DeMarco. "Four decades of trends in attitudes toward family issues in the United States: The 1960s through the 1990s." *Journal of Marriage and the Family*, vol. 63:4 (2001). 1009-1037.

20. *Fortune Magazine*, January 25, 2012, "Solo nation: American consumers stay single."

21. Ellwood, David T. and Christopher Jencks. "The Spread of Single-Parent Families in the United States Since 1960." John F. Kennedy School of Government, Harvard University, October 2002.

22. Jacobs, Andrew. "In China, myths of social cohesion." The *New York Times*, Aug. 18, 2014.

23. See cutting cords ceremony on page 133 in author's book *Dreams of the Reiki Shaman*.

CHAPTER 3

1. Pleck, Joseph H., Wellesley College Center for Research on Women, and Freya L. Sonenstein and Leighton C. Ku, Urban Institute. "Masculinity Ideology: Its Impact on Adolescent Males' Heterosexual Relationships." *Journal of Social Issues*. Vol. 49 (1993): pp. 11-29.

2. Ancona, Francesco Aristide. *Crisis in America: Father Absence.* Hauppauge, NY: Nova Science Publishers, 1998.

3. Blakenhorn, David. *Fatherless America.* New York: BasicBooks, 1995.

4. Putnam, Robert D. *Bowling Alone: The Collapse and Revival of American Community.* New York: Simon and Schuster, 2001.

5. "Growing number of dads home with the kids: Biggest increase among those caring for family." *Pew Research Social and Demographic Trends*, June 5, 2014.

6. Warren, Karen J., and Cady, Duane L., eds. *Bringing Peace Home: Feminism, Violence and Nature.* Bloomington and Indianapolis, IN: Indiana University Press, 1996.

7. Kuperberg, Arielle, Ph.D. "Does premarital cohabitation raise your

risk of divorce? "University *of North Carolina at Greensboro, Council on Contemporary Families, Brief Reports*. March 10, 2014. www. contemporaryfamilies.org.

8. "Debunked: Cohabitating couples not more likely to divorce," *USA Today*, March 11, 2014.

9. Kimmel, Michael. *Manhood in America: A Cultural History*. New York: Oxford University Press, 2012.

10. For more, see *The Righteous Mind: Why Good People Are Divided by Politics and Religion* by Jonathan Haidt. Reprint edition. New York: Vintage, 2013.

11. For more on how the original ideas of democracy in the United States were derived from Native societies, see Jean Houston's book, *Manual for the Peacemaker*.

12. See potlatch among Northwest tribes and "giveaway" ceremonies among Mississippian culture. In his book, *The Gift: The Form and Reason for Exchange in Archaic Societies*, (W.W. Norton, 2000; reprint, originally published, 1954), French ethnologist Marcel Mauss explores the custom from ancient Roman times through Native American societies.

Bibliography

Ancona, Francesco Aristide. *Crisis in America: Father Absence*. Hauppauge, NY: Nova Science Publishers, 1998.

Barthes, Roland. *Elements of Semiology*, trans. Annette Lavers and Colin Smith. New York: Hill and Wang, 1967.

Beattie, Melody. *Codependent No More: How to Stop Controlling Others and Start Caring for Your Self*. New York: Walker & Co., 1989.

Blakenhorn, David. *Fatherless America*. New York: BasicBooks, 1995.

Bly, Robert. *Iron John: A Book About Men*. Cambridge, MA: Da Capo Press, 2004.

Borg, Marcus J. *Meeting Jesus Again for the First Time*. New York: Harper San Francisco, 1995.

Boulter, Carmen. *Angels and Archetypes: An Evolutionary Map of Feminine Consciousness*. Rapid City, SD: Swan Raven, 1997.

Brokaw, Tom. *The Greatest Generation*. New York: Random House, 2001.

Castaneda, Carlos. *Tales of Power*. New York: Pocket Books, 1976.

Catches, Pete S., Sr., Peter V. Catches, ed. *Sacred Fireplace (Oceti Wakan): Life and Teachings of a Lakota Medicine Man*. Santa Fe, NM: Clear Light Publishers, 1999.

Connell, R. W. *Masculinities*. Berkeley: University of California Press, 2005.

Danielou, Alain, ed. *The Complete Kama Sutra: The First Unabridged Modern Translation of the Classic Indian Text*. Rochester, VT: Park Street, 1994.

Dreher, Henry. *Mind-Body Unity: A New Vision for Mind-Body Science and Medicine*. Baltimore: Johns Hopkins University Press, 2003

Eisler, Riane. *The Chalice and the Blade*. New York: HarperCollins, 1987.

——— . *The Real Wealth of Nations: Creating a Caring Economics*. San Francisco, CA: Barrett-Koehler, 2007.

Ewing, Jim PathFinder. *Clearing: A Guide to Liberating Energies Trapped in Buildings and Lands*. Forres, Scotland: Findhorn Press, 2006.

——— . *Finding Sanctuary in Nature: Simple Ceremonies in the Native American Tradition of Healing Yourself and Others*. Forres, Scotland: Findhorn Press, 2007.

——. *Healing Plants and Animals From a Distance: Curative Principles and Applications*. Forres, Scotland: Findhorn Press, 2007.

——. *Reiki Shamanism: A Guide to Out-of-Body Healing*. Forres, Scotland: Findhorn Press, 2008.

——. *Dreams of the Reiki Shaman: Expanding Your Healing Power*. Forres, Scotland: Findhorn Press, 2011.

——. *Conscious Food: Sustainable Growing, Spiritual Eating*. Forres, Scotland: Findhorn Press, 2012.

Farah, Caesar E. *Islam*, 6th Edition. Hauppauge, NY: Barron's Educational Series, 2000.

Friedman, Thomas L. *The World Is Flat A Brief History of the Twenty-First Century*. New York: Farrar, Straus and Giroux, 2005.

Funk, Robert W. *Honest to Jesus: Jesus For A New Millennium*. New York: HarperSanFrancisco, 1997.

Gray, John. *Mars and Venus on a Date*. New York: HarperCollins, 1997.

Gould, Joan. *Spinning Straw Into Gold: What Fairy Tales Reveal About the Transformations in a Woman's Life*. New York, Random House, 2006.

Haidt, Jonathan. *The Righteous Mind: Why Good People Are Divided by Politics and Religion*. New York: Vintage, 2013

Houston, Jean and Rubin, Margaret. *Manual for the Peacemaker: An Iroquois Legend to Heal Self and Society*. New York: Quest Books, 1994.

Houston, Jean. *The Possible Human: A Course in Enhancing Your Physical, Mental and Creative Abilities*. New York: Jeremy P. Tarcher/Putnam, 1982.

Hock, Ronald F. *The Infancy Gospels of James and Thomas: The Scholars Bible*. Santa Barbara, CA: Polebridge Press, 1995.

——. *The Life of Mary and the Birth of Jesus: The Ancient Infancy Gospel of James*. Berkeley, CA: Ulysses Press, 1997.

Ingerman, Sandra. *Medicine for the Earth: How to Transform Personal and Environmental Toxins*. New York: Three Rivers Press, 2000.

——. *Soul Retrieval: Mending the Fragmented Self*. San Francisco, CA: Harper, 1991.

Keen, Sam. *Fire in the Belly: On Being a Man*. New York: Bantam, 1992.

Kimmel, Michael. *Manhood in America: A Cultural History*. New York: Oxford University Press, 2012.

Lerman, Phil. *Daditude: How a Real Man Became a Real Dad*. Cambridge, MA: Da Dapo, 2007.

Lerner, Gerder. *The Creation of Patriarchy (Women and History, Vol 1)*. New York: Oxford University Press, 1987.

Maines, Rachel P. "The Technology of Orgasm: Hysteria" in *The Vibrator and Women's Sexual Satisfaction*. Baltimore, MD: Johns Hopkins University Press, 2001.

Mauss, Marcel. *The Gift: The Form and Reason for Exchange in Archaic Societies*. New York: W.W. Norton, 2000.

McElvaine, Robert S. *Eve's Seed: Biology, the Sexes and the Course of History*. New York: McGraw-Hill, 2000.

McFaddeen, Steven. *Profiles in Wisdom: Native Elders Speak About the Earth*. Santa Fe, NM: Bear & Co., 1991.

Medicine Eagle, Brooke. *The Last Ghost Dance: A Guide for Earth Mages*. New York: Wellspring/Ballantine, 2000.

——. *Buffalo Woman Comes Singing*. New York: Ballantine Books, 1991.

Melchizedek, Drunvalo. *Ancient Secrets of the Flower of Life*, vols. 1 and 2. Flagstaff, AZ: Light Technology Publishing, 1990.

Meyer, Marvin W. *The Secret Teachings of Jesus: Four Gnostic Gospels*. New York: Vintage Books, 1986.

Moore, Robert and Gillette, Douglas. *King, Lover, Magician, Lover: Rediscovering the Archetypes of the Mature Masculine*. New York: HarperCollins, 1990.

Muir, Charles and Caroline. *Tantra: The Art of Conscious Loving*. San Francisco, CA: Mercury House, 1989.

Northrup, Christiane, M.D. *Women's Bodies, Women's Wisdom: Creating Physical and Emotional Health and Healing*. Revised edition. New York: Bantam Books, 2010.

Pert, Candace B., Ph.D. *Molecules of Emotion: The Science Behind Mind-Body Medicine*. New York: Simon & Schuster, 1999.

Pesavento, Larry. *Toward Manhood: Into The Wilderness of the Soul*. Cincinnati, OH: Christos: A Center for Men, 2010.

Putnam, Robert D. *Bowling Alone: The Collapse and Revival of American Community*. New York: Simon and Schuster, 2001.

Quinn, Daniel. *Ishmael: An Adventure of the Mind and Spirit*. New York: Bantam Books, 1995.

Redmond, Layne. *When the Drummers Were Women: A Spiritual History of Rhythm*. New York: Three Rivers Press 1997.

Reeser, Todd W. *Masculinities in Theory: An Introduction*. Chichester, West Sussex, UK: John Wiley & Sons, 2010.

Robinson, James M., et al. *The Nag Hammadi Library*. New York: HarperSanFrancisco, 1990.

Rohr, Richard and Martos, Joseph. *From Wild Man to Wise Man: Reflections on Male Spirituality*. Cincinnati, OH: Franciscan Media, 2005.

Rosen, Hanna. *The End of Men: And the Rise of Women*. New York: Riverhead Books, 2012.

Stamper, Gary L. *Awakening The New Masculine: The Path of the Integral Warrior*. Bloomington, IN: iUniverse, 2012.

Sandberg, Sheryl. *Lean In: Women, Work, And the Will to Lead*. New York: Knopf, 2014.

Solnit, Rebecca. *Explain Things To Me*. New York: Haymarket, 2014.

Wall, Steve. *To Become a Human Being: The Message of Tadodaho Chief Leon Shenandoah*. Charlottesville, VA: Hampton Roads, 2001.

Wallace, Paul. *White Roots of Peace: The Iroquois Book of Life*. Santa Fe, NM: Clear Light Publishers, 1994.

Warren, Karen J., and Duane L. Cady, eds. *Bringing Peace Home: Feminism, Violence and Nature*. Bloomington and Indianapolis: Indiana University Press, 1996.

Welch, Bryan. *Beautiful and Abundant: Building the World We Want*. Lawrence, KS: B&A, 2010.

Whitfield, Charles L., M.D., *Boundaries and Relationships: Knowing, Protecting and Enjoying the Self*. Deerfield Beach, FL: Health Communications Inc, 1993.

Wilder, James E. *The Stages of a Man's Life*. Bolivar, MO: Quiet Waters Publications, 2003.

Wise, Michael, et al. *The Dead Sea Scrolls: A New Translation*. New York: HarperSanFrancisco, 1996.

Ywahoo, Dhyani. *Voices of the Ancestors: Cherokee Teachings from the Wisdom Fire*. Boston, MA: Shambhala Publications, 1987.

Acknowledgments

I am deeply thankful to my son Ross, his wife, Amber, and my grandson Nathan for their constant love and the joys they bring that helped prompt this book.

Special thanks goes to my friend Alison Buehler, who founded the Mississippi Modern Homestead Center, and persisted over three years to finally get me to write this book. (Yes, Alison, the workshop is on my calendar!) Thanks go also to Kripalu Center for Yoga & Health in Massachusetts for offering me a venue to teach my classes in a meditative and sacred space.

This book was greatly aided by the support of my ex-wife, sometimes work partner and BFF Annette, who provided the artwork, as in previous books, and helped me keep my spirits up when feeling overwhelmed or perplexed; to Nicky Leach, my editor, who has been a great wordsmith and advisor in this and in previous works; to Thierry Bogliolo at Findhorn Press, who thankfully backed this effort, along with my six previous books; and to Sabine, Carol, and the crew for their now-routine excellence in book production and promotion.

I am grateful to Jenna Ward for helping to keep me on track in the early stages of this book; to the crew at Lemuria Books, especially to Lisa for acting as a sounding board, and Maggie and Adie and John, for their friendship. Just being in that beautiful, independent bookstore (my home away from home) in Jackson, Mississippi, excites the muse to write;

To my buddy Joe Powell for being a guy, helpful and competitive, trustworthy and frank; to Rockiell Woods, a guy's guy, who women seem magically attracted to, and good friend who makes me laugh and can help fill a delightful afternoon talking sports, women, and so on, and just looking at tools and stuff; to my old hunting and fishing partners of days of yore; and to all the guys I've had the pleasure and misfortune to learn from, including my longtime best friend Peter Bloom, and my now-long-distance bud Boe Glasschild. Here's to our times as the three amigos, may the tales of bravery and derring-do they engendered live forever in the lives of, um, us.

Thanks to my mother and father and my sister for the formative years and constant refinement of family dynamics over the decades.

Of course, my gratitude is overflowing for the opportunities I had while serving as a spiritual and ceremonial elder for our beloved but now defunct Southern Cherokee Tribe & Associated Bands in Texas, as well as other organizations where it was my duty to counsel couples and perform marriages; and although I am mostly retired from active energy work, to the many clients I have had over the years.

I am grateful to a succession of wives, lovers, and girlfriends who have schooled me on male-female relationships in ways as soft as a kiss and as hard as a mallet on meat. Their love—bitter and sweet, hot and cold—has made life delicious.

About the Author

Jim PathFinder Ewing (Nvnehi Awatisgi) is a writer, editor, and author, a former organic farmer, and a Reiki Master teacher who also teaches shamanism. He travels extensively, giving workshops, classes, and lectures. For more information, visit his website at *www.blueskywaters.com*.

FINDHORN PRESS

Life-Changing Books

Consult our catalogue online
(with secure order facility) on
www.findhornpress.com

For information on the Findhorn Foundation:
www.findhorn.org